FAMILY TREES

A Manual for their
Design, Layout & Display

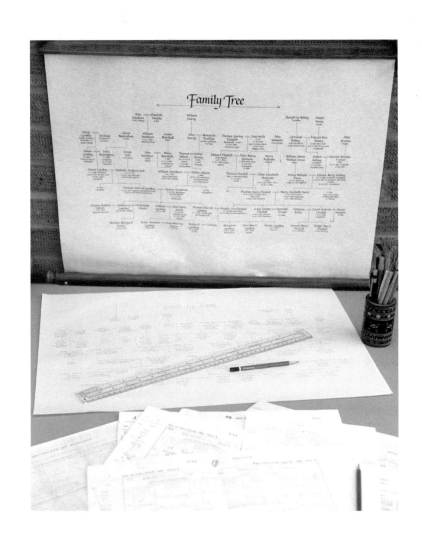

FAMILY TREES

A Manual for their
Design, Layout & Display

◆

Marie Lynskey

Phillimore

1996

Published by
PHILLIMORE & CO. LTD.
Shopwyke Manor Barn, Chichester, West Sussex

ISBN 0 85033 980 4

Printed and bound in Great Britain by
LAWRENCE-ALLEN LTD.
Weston-super-Mare, Avon

Contents

Foreword

by

Cecil R. Humphery-Smith, FSA, FSG, FHS
Principal of The Institute of Heraldic and Genealogical Studies

Genealogy has had a huge revival in popularity in recent years and one in which Common Man has had an opportunity to compare his pedigree with those of the armigerous landed gentry. Compiled, beautifully scrivened and illuminated in the sixteenth and later centuries, these family trees used to hang over fireplaces in country houses. The desire to display ancestry seems to increase proportionately with the uncertainty of the Age, but that is balanced by an increasing appreciation of the value of the cultural past.

Matters of balance and proportion concern calligraphers. One recalls being taught the rudimentary principles of layout and of balancing slopes and extents of ascending and descending strokes, of ensuring that spaces and holes were equal, all of which has been conveyed to subsequent generations of calligraphers.

Of those who practise the craft today, Marie Lynskey is surely one of the most talented. Above all she has that essential sense of design that makes her productions of family trees into works of art. Like all enthusiasts, Marie wants to share her skills. In *Family Tree Design*, she does just that with the added qualities of a good teacher. In these well-ordered pages is entertaining and comprehensive instruction which had been wanting.

Cecil R. Humphery-Smith.

Chapter 1
Where to Start?

Genealogy is a fascinating hobby and one which is becoming increasingly popular. There are many publications available which give advice on how to research your family history, but this book is an attempt to give instruction in the actual production of a well thought out, attractive chart as an end product of all your research. For those starting from scratch, however, this first chapter briefly outlines how to assemble family details and set off on a discovery of the family history.

The most important thing to remember when planning to draw up a family tree chart is to collect together your information in a clear and well organised way. Whether you are just beginning, with all your research ahead of you, or whether you need to sift what you have already gathered into the material you want to show on your chart, the initial steps are the same. No matter what eventual layout you choose to use for the final copy, a well organised layout will save a lot of confusion and possible mistakes at a later stage.

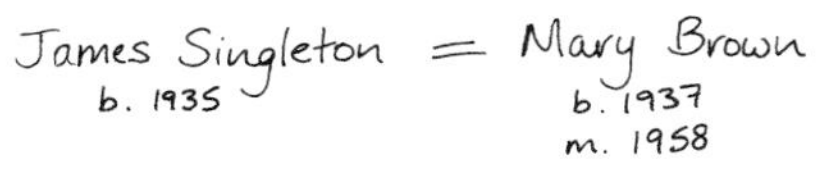

Begin on a large sheet of paper with the details of your immediate family and put together the information for a husband and wife as shown in fig. 1. It is best to write the name of a person in a larger lettering size than any further details as this makes the chart easier to follow. An = sign is used to link a married couple and from this can descend the line on which the children appear as shown in fig. 2a. Many people like to use an 'm' to link a married couple rather than the = sign and this is perfectly satisfactory; however, the = sign has the advantage of connecting conveniently with the line down to the children. If you wish to show unions without marriage then two wavy or zigzagging lines can be used instead of the straight lines (fig. 2b).

This is the basis of a drop-line pedigree and on the whole it is the clearest, simplest and most attractive method of laying out a family tree. Each family group of parents and children is linked together in the same manner, and all the children of a couple should be kept on the same level in a row so that it is obvious to which generation they belong. Working backwards, forwards or out to the sides from the initial information, the chart grows;

Fig. 1 Linking a married couple

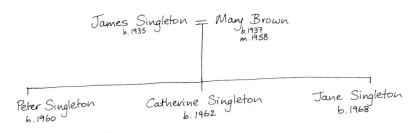

Fig. 2a Adding the children

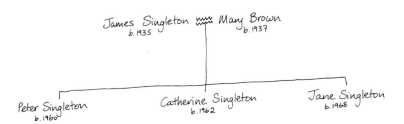

Fig. 2b Unmarried couples

and you should always try to keep an entire generation on the same level across the page. It is a good idea to rule light horizontal lines right across the page (fig. 3) to use as guide lines for placing other members of the family in line. If, when you are mapping out your chart, you allow the generations to become out of step as in fig. 4a this will lead to much confusion later on. On a very complex chart it is sometimes necessary to step one or two people in a generation out of line (this will be explained later in 'Problem Solving') but it should be avoided whenever possible as it makes the chart much more difficult to read and leads to design problems. The misaligned areas in 4a are shown corrected in 4b.

It is normal practice to place the husband to the left-hand side and the wife to the right of the marriage sign but this arrangement is not always practicable. Where you have a choice, therefore, keep to the preferred order, but if the content of your chart makes this arrangement unsatisfactory, then it is not 'wrong' to place the names the other way round. There is no right or wrong way of laying out a pedigree; the only rule you need to apply is that it should be clear and easy to follow.

Second marriages are easily dealt with by placing, for example, two wives to either side of the husband. Make sure to put the first wife to the left-hand side if possible, as this will ensure that the children will appear in chronological order underneath (fig. 5). If there is a third or even a fourth marriage, the layout often becomes a little difficult but various ways of overcoming this and other sorts of complication are shown in chapter 3.

It does not matter under which name of a married couple the marriage details are listed. It makes sense to place the details under the family member rather than under the person marrying into the family, whether male or female, but in general, for the purposes of clarity, it is

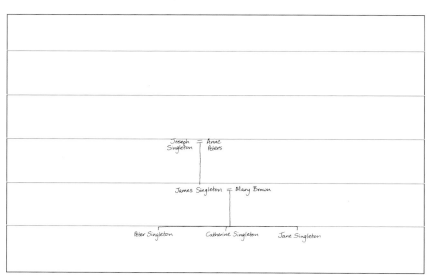

Fig. 3 Ruling horizontal guidelines

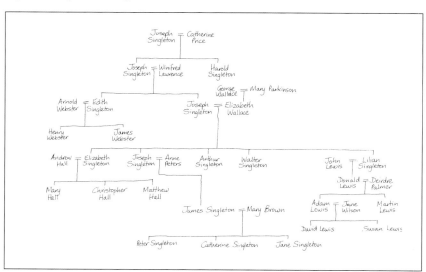

Fig. 4a Roughly plotted notes

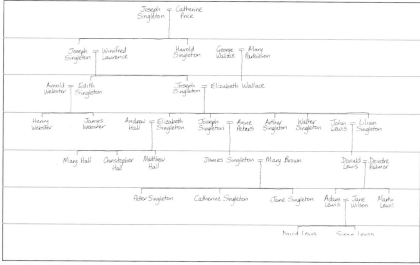

Fig. 4b Well organised notes

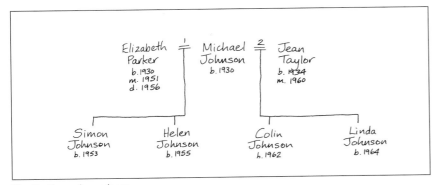

Fig. 5 Second marriages

Fig. 6 Using imaginary boxes around text

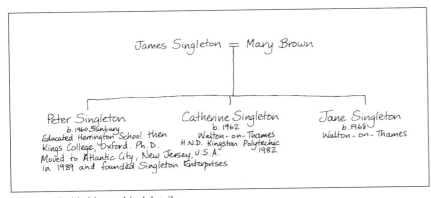

Fig. 7a Untidy biographical details

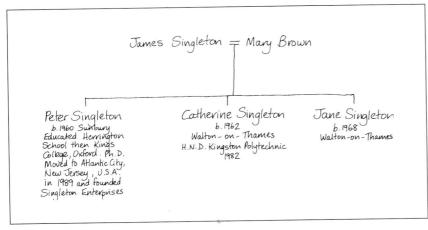

Fig. 7b Well placed biographical details.

preferable to put these details under whichever person has the least other information. Centre the information beneath the name, if possible, and as you add further information try to keep within an imaginary box (fig. 6) around the name so that you achieve a neat appearance and avoid the danger of overlapping with another person. There is a great tendency when adding additional notes to tack them on in such a way that it can be very difficult to tell exactly to which person they refer (fig. 7a). The best way of avoiding this sort of muddle is to leave plenty of space around any person about whom you are likely to want to give a lot of detail. Fig. 7b shows how the information in fig. 7a should be rearranged.

You will quickly build up a chart of your near family from your own memory. The next step is to ask your relatives. If you decide to try to include every relative you will probably end up with a chart about five times as wide as it is high. If you like the idea of making a chart to contain this sort of information, it can be done very well but requires some extra thought in the layout to avoid a very wide and shallow chart. If you want to go more into the history and origins of the family, go straight to your older relatives.

An important thing to remember with older relatives, who will be trying to remember things from many years back, is that, however good their memories might be, the information cannot be regarded as totally correct until verified with definite proof. Use the information given as pointers to the records themselves which will tell you with certainty the names, places and dates you are searching for. Do not be content with a chart hastily put together, which bears a reasonable affinity to the truth but which is by no means entirely accurate. There is a possibility that this set of information will be passed on in the future and regarded as correct when it is not a faithful portrait of events. If you are given information about which you are not sure, then make a note on the chart to that effect so that you are always aware that it could be incorrect.

Once you have exhausted the memories of those willing to assist you in your research and have rummaged very thoroughly through the family papers, you will need to start consulting record repositories. The first port of call is St Catherine's House in London, the home of the birth, marriage and death records since 1837 in England. If you are lucky enough to come through this ordeal with a full set of ancestors back to the commencement of the records, this is an achievement in itself as there are many problems to be encountered on the way, such as ancestors who for one reason or another escaped registration. However, progress can be very quick and satisfying if you are prepared to spend some time searching through the large index books. The full address is given in the list on page 5.

The sources of information available to genealogists after St Catherine's House are many and varied. There are dozens of excellent research guides available to point you in the right direction. As this book is mainly concerned with the layout rather than the content of your chart I will go no further into research in these pages than to list opposite a few of the repositories to which you will probably next have recourse.

What to include?

If you have been working on your family history for some time, you will probably have amassed quite a lot of material and will need to decide just what to include on the chart and what to leave out.

Decide what you would like to say about each person. You will almost certainly want to include a series of dates if known, of principal events such as birth, marriage, death, baptism, burial. You may

wish to include occupations, towns lived in, academic careers, honours awarded. Finally you may want to write in particularly interesting anecdotes relating to individuals. If you are planning a chart including a great deal of biographical information, you will probably need to use a set of abbreviations.

Abbreviations

There is no fixed system of abbreviations in genealogy, but the list opposite contains those most frequently used by genealogists. Many genealogists have adopted their own system during years of research, so this is by no means the only correct set of abbreviations, but it is a system which works well and is a good starting point.

Once the content of the chart has been decided the next thing to consider is what you will use in its construction.

Materials

The first thing to decide upon is the surface on which you will carry out the work. This is the sort of document that you will want to keep in the family for many years, so it is worth taking the trouble to acquire good quality materials which will produce good results and which will stand the test of time.

Paper – A strong, good quality paper does not cost a great deal and will give you a much better chance of producing an attractive document. There are specialist paper shops in many towns and some supply papers by mail order, so it should not be too difficult to obtain something suitable. The qualities you need to look for in a paper are 1) a good, smooth surface which will absorb the ink but not allow it to spread; 2) an ability to withstand the removal of incorrect letters, therefore fairly thick and not damaged by rough usage; 3) good ageing potential;

Repositories

General Register Office,
St. Catherine's House,
10 Kingsway,
London. WC2B 6JP   Tel. (0171) 242 0262

Births, marriages and deaths registered in England and Wales since 1837. Various other records of services etc.

Principal Registry of the Family Division
Somerset House
The Strand
London. WC2R 1LP   Tel. (0171) 936 6000

Wills which have been proved or administrations granted from 1858 to the present. Administrations contain little of use but wills can give a wealth of information on whole families. Divorce registry.

The Land Registry,
Portugal Street,
London.   Tel. (0171) 917 8888

This building is part of the Public Record Office and houses the census returns from 1841 onwards. These records of the population, taken every 10 years, contain the names and addresses of everybody on the night that the census was taken and can be very useful for listing whole families.

County Record Offices

All English Counties have at least one County Record Office and these contain many deposited records of use to family historians such as parish records, wills, marriage licence records etc.

The Society of Genealogists,
14 Charterhouse Buildings,
Goswell Road,
London. EC1M 7BA   Tel. (0171) 251 8799

Large library of genealogical material, publications, research advice

Parish Records

Parish records are records of birth, marriage and death kept by individual parishes and from varying dates of commencement. Many have been deposited in County Record Offices but sometimes it may be necessary to visit the area concerned to see the records at first hand.

Federation of Family History Societies,
The Administrator,
Benson Room,
Birmingham & Midland Institute,
Margaret Street,
Birmingham B3 3BS

There are now many family history societies throughout the country and it is well worth getting in touch with those in the area about which you are concerned. Most publish journals containing much of interest to researchers and, more importantly, the addresses of other researchers who may have a common interest.

National and Local Libraries

The resources of public libraries can be very great for genealogists and the material is usually available for consultation free of charge. Many local libraries have good local studies sections containing parish register copies, old newspapers, etc. Large national libraries also contain much useful information.

The Institute of Heraldic and
   Genealogical Studies
Northgate,
Canterbury CT1 1BA Tel. (01227) 768664

Extensive library and training resources; full/part-time and correspondence courses of instruction.

Basic abbreviations

bap.	baptised	gent.	gentleman	pr.	proved
b.	born	gfr.	grandfather	s. & h.	son and heir
bur.	buried	ggfr.	great grandfather	unm.	unmarried
chr.	christened	k.	killed	w.	will
dau.	daughter	m.	married	w.p.	will proved
d.	died	nat.	natural (illegitimate)		
div	divorced		son/daughter		

Latin terms

d.s.p.	decessit sine prole	died without issue
ob.	obiit	died
c.	circa	approximately

Record Offices, etc.

B.L.	British Library
D.N.B.	Dictionary of National Biography
Co.	County
C.R.O.	County Record Office
F.H.S.	Family History Society
G.R.O.	General Register Office
I.G.I.	International Genealogical Index
M.I.	Monumental Inscription
MS	Manuscript
P.C.C.	Prerogative Court of Canterbury
P.C.Y.	Prerogative Court of York
R.D.	Registration District
TS	Typescript
V.C.H.	Victoria County Histories

4) an attractive appearance which will enhance the work. Size could also be a factor if you intend to produce a large chart.

Good quality white cartridge paper is readily available in most art shops and stationers. Ingres paper is also very widely available and this comes in a large range of colours. The paper has a grained or laid surface which looks very attractive and is perfectly good for writing on; one of its drawbacks is that it is a little thin. Canson 'Mi-Teintes' paper is now becoming widely available in art shops in a wide range of colours and this is an excellent paper for family trees. The sheets are quite large, measuring 75cm x 55cm, and the paper takes alterations very well. The surface is slightly more coarse than cartridge and Ingres paper, but it should present no problems to the careful writer. This paper is also available in large rolls 150cm wide and 10 metres long which should cater for the largest charts! Another very good paper is Fabriano paper, which comes in a variety of surfaces for different uses. Some cheaper papers can age very quickly, becoming yellow and brittle, so if you want to ensure that your chart will be in good condition in many years time buy an archive quality paper. Consult the supplier and explain your requirements; good paper shops know what qualities their papers have.

It is worth thinking about hand-made paper for your chart. It has several advantages over machine-made paper, the principal one being that it has a lot of strength, both vertically and horizontally, due to its manufacture. Machine-made papers tend to have all the fibres lying in the same direction which means that in one direction the paper will tear more easily. Chatsworth Vellum is a hand-made paper which is made to resemble vellum and has a very good surface; it is a little more expensive than most of the machine-made papers mentioned. T.H. Saunders paper is a type you might find in art shops.

It is white or slightly off-white and comes in a selection of different surfaces.

Whatever paper you decide to use, it is important to try it out first before committing yourself to using it for the work. Give a sheet a thorough testing by writing some sample sentences on it, as you sometimes find with modern machine-made papers that the surface is not even throughout. You can start writing beautifully only to find that the ink suddenly hits a porous patch and spreads out, giving you fat furry letters. Take care, if you find this happens to you, that it really is the paper that is at fault and not where you have inadvertently spoilt it with careless finger marks making greasy patches.

An increasing range of papers is coming onto the market which attempt to imitate parchment and vellum; these will be dealt with after the genuine material has been explained.

Parchment and Vellum – The traditional surface on which valuable documents are produced is vellum or parchment. These materials are the skins of animals which have been specially cleaned and treated and which have been used for writing since medieval times until the Chinese invention of paper reached us. They are still produced and are used for valuable documents which need to stand the passage of many years. The cost of these materials is very high and they are not recommended for first attempts but as something to use when you are confident that you are prepared to spend a lot of time and effort in producing an article of which you can be proud for years to come.

Vellum is the skin of calves and parchment is the skin of sheep. Goat skin is also used. Vellum is the superior material as it is stronger and thicker and can withstand harsher treatment than parchment. The skins are sold whole by the square foot, or cut sizes can be bought. Offcuts are also available so you can try

Fig. 8 Vellum and a selection of papers: Canson Mi-Teintes, Fabriano, Chatsworth vellum, Marlmarque, Parchmarque.

them out before committing yourself to the expense of a large piece. A good sized skin of vellum (about eight square feet) will cost about £80 and a skin of parchment £40. The skins can be purchased already prepared for writing and they are called manuscript vellum.

If you decide to use vellum for your chart, you will also need to buy a powder called 'pounce', which is the substance used by vellum manufacturers to make the surface smooth and suitable for writing. It is made up of very finely ground pumice stone, cuttlefish and other substances which help to improve the quality of the skin. Although the manuscript vellum you buy has already been prepared for writing, you will often find, as you handle the skin whilst measuring and cutting, that the surface loses some of its quality which can then be restored with the pounce powder. It always pays to repounce completely the surface before you draw up your writing lines and begin the text, as you will find that your text will be much more precise if the skin surface is correct. To apply the powder you will need a spare offcut of the vellum, about six by four inches. Place your cut piece of vellum on a large sheet of paper and sprinkle a small quantity of powder over the surface. Rub the powder into the vellum with the spare piece and work in circular movements all over the skin. It is important that you get a uniform surface with no particular direction for the nap of the vellum. (The nap is the slight texture given to the vellum by the fibres which protrude slightly from the surface.) A slight nap is required for writing as the pen and ink will bite into the surface better, but do not overdo it and make the surface too coarse. Rub over the whole surface for about five to seven minutes. You need to apply a reasonable amount of pressure as you rub so it is quite tiring. Watch the surface carefully to see how the nap is looking; if you think you have made it a little too rough then stop. You will be able to see how you can rub too much from

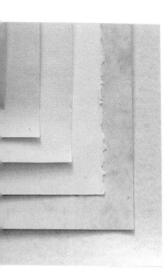

the state of the scrap piece being used for the rubbing. This will become quite worn as the same spot is used constantly. It is unlikely that you will do any damage to a skin in five minutes if you are rubbing over the whole area. When you have finished, pick up the skin and shake off the excess powder; you can also dust it very lightly with tissue so that not too much powder residue remains. You can now begin working on the vellum. Parchment and goatskin must be pounced much more carefully than vellum. Rub in the powder with a light pressure and only for a very short time, watching very carefully that the surface does not become too coarse. Suppliers of vellum and pounce are listed at the back of the book. Documents written on vellum are shown in figs. 36, 56, 88c, 107, 109 and 121.

Imitation parchment abounds now, especially as an accompaniment to calligraphy equipment, which is produced in great quantities now that the hobby has become so popular. Many of these papers should be treated with extreme caution as they are not often suitable for finished work. They take the form of rather flimsy, sometimes slightly transparent, pale cream coloured papers and are often described as parchment although they are nothing of the sort. These types of paper should be avoided or used only for rough work. There are some very good parchment-effect papers which are well worth searching out. 'Parchmarque' and 'Marlmarque' are two very attractive papers available in various colours. They also come in two thicknesses and the thicker is recommended.

Writing Instruments

It is not necessary to be an accomplished calligrapher to produce good clear lettering on a family tree. Calligraphy simply means 'beautiful writing' and, if your own handwriting is attractive enough to give your chart a pleasing appearance, then you need delve no further into that artform; but for those who wish to have a go at a more formalised lettering for their chart I have included a brief run-through of various methods of achieving good results.

Most art shops and many stationers sell good calligraphy pens and the best ones to use are the William Mitchell series (fig. 9). The nibs come in a variety of styles and sizes separate from the pen holders so that you can change them around. A small reservoir fits over the nib and holds the ink in place. Roundhand nibs are the ones recommended for the lettering styles most suitable for family trees. Buy a selection of sizes, they are quite cheap, so that you can experiment and choose those which will best suit the work.

It is very important to choose a good ink, no matter what sort of pen you have chosen. Many inks fade with age, some disappearing almost entirely when exposed to constant daylight, so try to find one which will not do so. The best ink to use is Chinese stick ink, which needs to be ground on an ink slate with water until the required strength is reached (see fig. 10a). This ink will not fade over the years whether on a document rolled up

Fig. 9 Calligraphy pens

and stored away in an attic or displayed on the wall for all to see. With a proper calligraphy pen such as the William Mitchell type, the ink is applied between the nib and the reservoir with a small paint brush. The pen must be washed after use as the ink dries solid and is not easily removed. It is possible to buy chinese ink in liquid form and this is usually very good, although the preservatives used in it prevent the strokes from being quite as crisp as those which can be obtained with freshly ground ink. Many of the pens sold for calligraphy require cartridges. The ink in cartridges is often of very poor quality but Rotring make cartridges for their 'Artpen' range in which the quality of the ink is very good. The ink is a good strong black and is more lightfast than most other types. These cartridges are a standard size that will fit most pens. Rotring also produce a range of coloured ink cartridges. Do bear in mind, if you decide to use ordinary fountain pen ink, the strong possibility that the ink will fade. If the work will not be on show in daylight, then this might be adequate for your needs, but give the matter much thought if you intend to display the work on the wall.

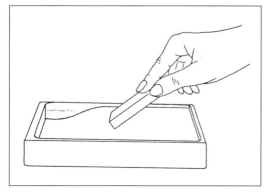

Fig. 10a Grinding stick ink with water in an ink slate

Fig. 10b Inks and paints

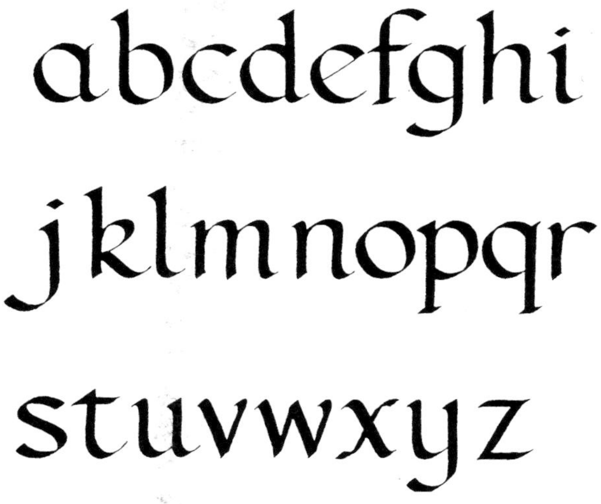

Paint can often be preferable to bad ink and you then have a choice of any colour you can mix. Winsor and Newton's 'Designers Gouache' writes beautifully in a William Mitchell nib. You will need to take care to wash the nib frequently, as the paint will dry and clog slightly as you work, but the results are very good. However, many colours of paint are not lightfast; the tube usually indicates the permanence of the colour, so try to avoid those which are not good in this respect (fig. 10b).

The foundation hand or roundhand alphabet is what most calligraphers learn first and its simplicity and clarity make it a perfect choice for family trees. Clarity is the most important factor on a family pedigree and, although there are many other attractive lettering styles which can be used effectively on pedigrees, they should not be employed at the expense of legibility. The roundhand alphabets are shown in figures 11a and b. The height of the letters in this alphabet should be five times the width of the nib you have chosen. It is sensible to write between guidelines no matter what sort of lettering you intend to use. You should also measure the distance between each set of writing lines so that it is consistent throughout the work. All these considerations will enhance the overall appearance of your chart.

Alternatives to calligraphy equipment which produce good results are Rotring technical pens. These pens are precision drawing instruments which produce a fine even line of a consistent width. They are available in a range of sizes down to one producing a very fine line 0.10mm thick. With a Rotring pen you will not be able to make letters which graduate from thick to thin in stroke as calligraphic edged pens do, but if you have a steady hand and patience you should be able to produce neat attractive lettering which will age well. An alphabet written with a size 0.35mm Rotring pen is shown in fig. 12.

abcdefghi jklmnopqr stuvwxyz

Fig. 11a Roundhand minuscules

ABCDEFGHI JKLMNOPQ RSTUVWXYZ

Fig. 11b Roundhand majuscules

9

Stencils are another method of producing neat lettering for those unwilling to rely on their own hand-writing. Provided care is taken in the drawing of accurate guidelines, the effect of stencilled lettering can be very attractive. Many shops sell lettering stencils but in general they are too large for family trees. Rotring produce a series of stencils for use with their technical pens. Both upright and italic alphabets are available and the lettering produced can be very attractive if carefully drawn. It is necessary to buy a stencil which matches the pen size you will use. A piece of lettering using the type of stencil shown in fig. 13 is illustrated in fig. 14.

Transfer lettering could be considered if you fail in all your other attempts to produce good lettering. There are many attractive lettering styles available in transfer form and they are very easy, albeit a little time consuming, to apply. Sets can be purchased in upright, italic and gothic styles.

Drawing Board

The most comfortable way to write is on a sloping surface and you will be able to produce better results if you work on the chart with your paper at the correct angle of slope. If you do not have a purpose-made drawing board then try to find a good sized piece of 10mm-thick ply board or fibre board (available from hardware shops) about three by two feet. The board should be at an angle of about 45 degrees, but if this is not possible try to slope the board by propping it up at one end, when it rests on a table. You can rest the board on your lap and against a table, but this is uncomfortable for long periods and impractical if the board is large. You should use as large a board as you can manage—to work on a large piece of paper on a small board is very awkward.

a b c d e f g h i j k l m n o p q r s t u v w x y z

James Singleton ══ Mary Brown

Fig. 12 Rotring pen lettering

Fig. 13 Rotring pen and lettering stencil

ABCDEFGHIJKLMNOPQRSTUVWXYZ
abcdefghijklmnopqrstuvwxyz

ABCDEFGHIJKLMNOPQRSTUVWXYZ

abcdefghijklmnopqrstuvwxyz

1234567890

Peter Robertson ══ Jean Davis
m. 15 June 1972

Fig. 14 Stencilled lettering

James Singleton ══ Mary Brown

James Singleton ══ Mary Brown

Fig. 15 Transfer lettering

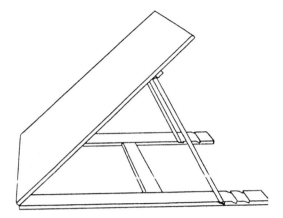

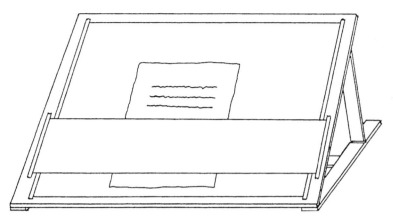

Fig. 16 Drawing board at correct
angle and with guard sheet

When you are working on the final document you should touch the work surface as little as possible. Hands transmit a certain amount of grease and dirt onto the paper and too much grease might impair the lettering, if you need to write over the affected area. It is therefore a good idea to attach a guard sheet to the drawing board as shown in fig. 16, so that you can insert the paper underneath it and write with your hand resting on the guard

sheet. The part of the page you are about to write on is exposed just above the top edge of the guard sheet; as you write each line the page can be moved up. If your sheet of paper is too large for you to attach a guard sheet to the board, then use a free moving sheet placed beneath your hands and arms to prevent them resting on the page. A large sheet of blotting paper is ideal as a guard sheet.

The connecting lines

Apart from the lettering, the chart will contain a network of lines connecting the information. The best method of drawing these lines is with a ruling pen (see fig. 17). These are available from art shops and stationers. The tip of the pen can be adjusted to determine the width of line produced. Ink or paint is put into the gap between the two halves and the line is drawn along the edge of a ruler. Alternatively a Rotring pen and ruler can be used.

Once you are armed with all the information on your family you can find and are equipped with the necessary materials for the work, the task of accurate layout begins.

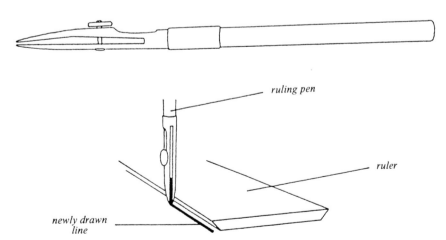

ruling pen

ruler

newly drawn line

Fig. 17 Ruling pen and how it is used

Chapter 2
Layout

There are many different methods of laying out the information on a family tree. For a start you have to decide on the general appearance – very simple and straightforward with no unnecessary embellishment; or an elaborate highly decorated work of art with lots of illustrations. Charts can run from top to bottom, left to right or even in semi-circular or circular format. You can choose to concentrate on a single line of descent or perhaps to incorporate all the text within a neat framework of boxes. Some of the more elaborate forms of layout will be dealt with in chapter 6, but this chapter will deal with upright charts using text and connecting lines only.

Drop-line Pedigrees

Drop-line pedigrees require a great deal of care in the layout to give a clear, well balanced result. Unless you want to produce a direct line of descent only or a birth brief type of layout, the chart will follow the construction of your own particular family; it is your job to make sure that the information is arranged in the best manner possible so that it is both clearly readable and attractive.

To illustrate the steps in the production of a typical drop-line chart of six generations of one family, the information in fig.18 will be used. This has been prepared in draft form following the guidelines in the previous chapter. It is important to lay out your draft clearly in this manner first, so that you can see

Fig. 18 Pedigree details before layout begins

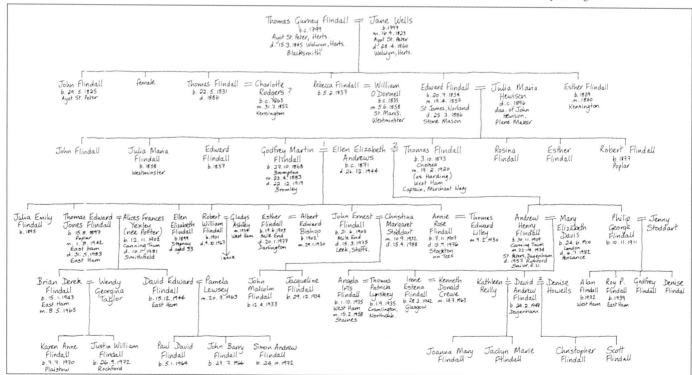

exactly how many generations deep the chart is and how many people there are in each generation.

Choosing lettering sizes

To determine the overall dimensions of your chart you need to choose the sizes of lettering you will use. Experiment by writing a few of the names in a line with your chosen writing instrument to see how much space they occupy. You should be

Fig. 19   Width of writing lines for calligraphic pens

Fig. 20   Sample widths of writing lines for other pens

able to tell if you have chosen a size which would make the chart much too large when all the names are written. There is no fixed set of sizes for a chart; the size will depend on the amount of information to be included. Small charts can obviously be written in larger lettering sizes where there is less to fit in. On a very large chart you will probably have to write in the smallest size that you can manage, to fit everything onto your paper. Use a larger lettering size for the names and a smaller sized lettering for the biographical details so that the names will stand out, making the chart easier to follow. It is best to make a reasonable difference in the two sizes. With William Mitchell pens a good starting point is a nib size 4 for the names and a size 5 for the smaller details (fig. 19). With other pens a good guide is writing lines of 4mm apart for the larger

text and 2mm apart for the smaller text (fig. 20). Some people can write very well on a single writing line but two are safer to be sure of producing even lettering, and you will soon get used to making the letters touch both lines without overlapping. Try various different combinations of lettering size until you have found those that you think will work best.

Spacing the generations

To some extent a chart establishes its own dimensions because of its content but you do have control over the overall size and shape by adjusting the amount of space in and around each person and generation on the chart.

Taking, for example, the information in fig.18, the general shape is already established as landscape rather than portrait shape (that is, the page will be wider than it is high) but, if you were set on having a portrait-shaped chart, perhaps to fit the spot on the wall you have chosen for the finished chart, then you can alter the spacing of the whole piece, as shown in fig. 21, to give you the desired shape.

This is an extreme example to show how a chart can be totally reshaped. Usually you will just want to adjust the spacing sufficiently to give you a chart with good proportions – neither too long and narrow nor too square. You can use spacing to give a better balance between generations that are sparse and those that are crowded. The third generation, for example, has far fewer names than the fourth or fifth, so those in the third row can be spaced widely apart whilst those in the fifth row must be placed as closely together as possible. This gives these two lines less disparate widths and will avoid large areas of empty space on the chart.

Most charts look better for having each generation spaced at the same distance apart. Taking a large sheet of

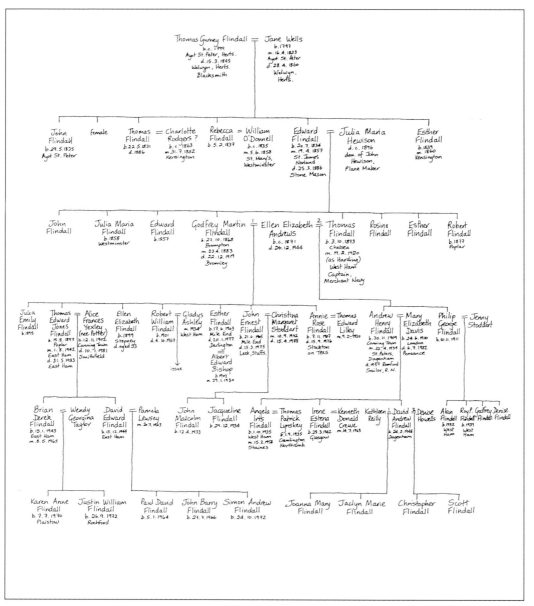

Fig. 21 Portrait arrangement of rough notes

Fig. 22 Ruling horizontal guidelines

layout paper (thin drafting paper available in pads from art shops) at least A2 (594mm x 420mm) in size, estimate a width for the distance apart that you would like the generations to be. For the sample chart 5cm has been chosen, as this will give a reasonable amount of space in which to fit any biographical details without leaving too much vacant space between each generation. Horizontal lines are therefore ruled at 5cm apart down the page for the number of generations to be included (fig. 22).

Thomas Gurney Flindall

Thomas Gurney
Flindall

Thomas
Gurney
Flindall

Fig. 23 Different arrangements of names

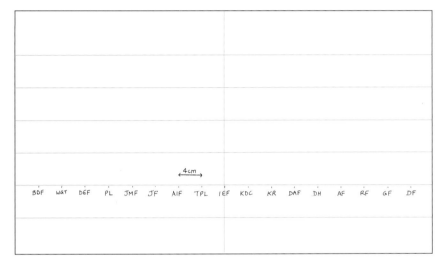

Fig. 24 Plotting the first row of names

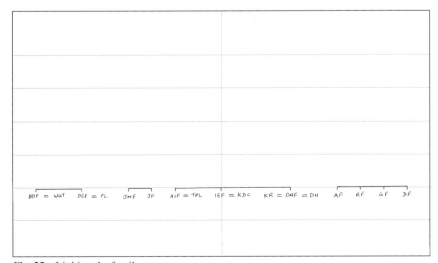

Fig. 25 Linking the family groups

Spacing the names

Count up the number of names in each generation and make a note of them. The generation to work with first is the widest with the most names – in this case the fifth generation. If this line of names will fit onto the page using the lettering sizes you have chosen, then all the rest will. If you find that you cannot make all the names fit, you can either increase the size of paper or decrease the lettering sizes. Write out a few of the names to see how much space you need to allow for each person. They can be written on two or three lines, rather than a single line, to save space (fig.23). For example, names on the top three generations will probably need only one or two lines but, where space is more confined on the lower generations, three or more lines will be needed wherever there are long names.

When you have a rough idea of the amount of space to allow for each person, draw a vertical line down the middle of the page so that you can divide the names in each generation evenly to either side of the centre, and this will enable you to see where the middle names in each row should fall. Mark off, along the horizontal line representing the relevant generation on your layout sheet, the number of people in that generation, arranging them equally to left and right of the centre vertical line. You can pencil in the initials of each person under each mark so that you don't lose track of who goes where. If the line contains an odd number of names then the centre name will fall across the middle line of the page as in the sample chart. If you have an even number of names then space the two centre names to either side of the centre line. On the example chart four centimetres was allowed for each name (fig. 24).

Pencil in the marriage (=) signs for any couples and link together families of brothers and sisters as shown (fig.25).

Follow the same process for each generation. You will need to add lines connecting parents to children as shown in fig. 26. If you are lucky and your chart is not too complex, all the vertical connecting lines will join up to the correct family groups in the underneath generation. If you have several large families, then very often, as in the example, the children do not fall directly beneath the parents, so you have to take the connecting line down from the parents = sign then along parallel but just above the other intervening families on the line until it can drop down and meet up with the right children. If you mean to include a lot of biographical detail with some of the people on your chart, you should bear in mind that the amount of space available for this reduces with each one of these parallel lines. Sometimes it is necessary to run two or three lines in parallel for some distance, so in order to fit in all your notes you might have to increase the space between each generation, making the whole chart deeper.

As you work through the generations you will find that the names on those with fewer numbers of people can be spaced wider apart. The third generation in the example-chart has far fewer names than the fourth or fifth, so the names have been placed at six centimetres apart (fig. 27). The top two generations on this chart were fairly straightforward and could be treated in the same way but the bottom generation was approached slightly differently.

It is preferable to have an even balance of names to left and right of the page so that the chart has a symmetrical appearance. But there is no point in placing children too far from their parents, with long connecting lines, if this is not absolutely necessary. Once the longest generation has been established and plotted you can be more flexible with subsequent shorter ones so that they fall in a more advantageous position. If the final row of names in the example were centred (see fig. 28), the lines from the parents would be unnecessarily long. It is

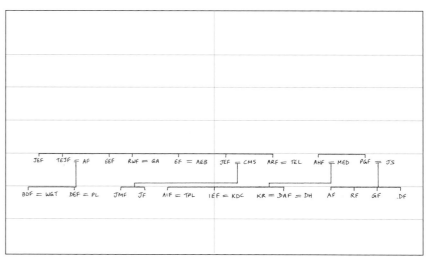

Fig. 26   Plotting the next generation

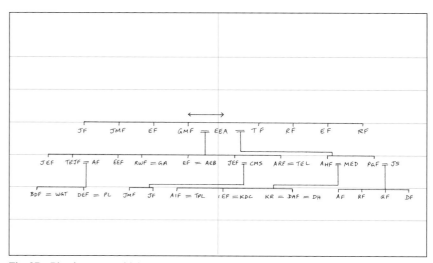

Fig. 27   Plotting more widely spaced generations

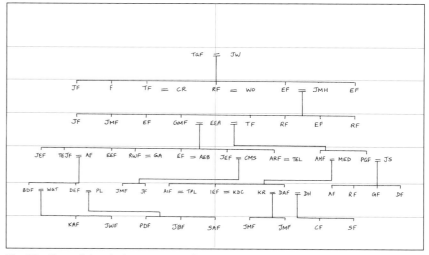

Fig. 28   Centralising the bottom generation

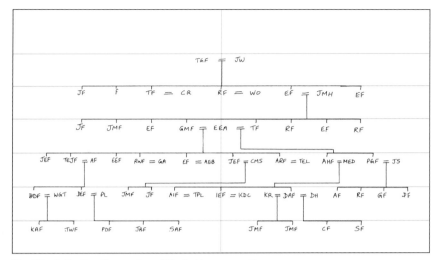

Fig. 29   Adjusting the spacing of the bottom generation

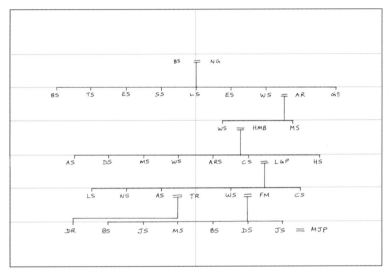

Fig. 30   Positioning narrow generations

Writing the names in rough and positioning

When you have marked out the positions of all the members of the family, it is necessary to write out all the names in rough to ensure that they will fit and that you will be able to write each name on the finished piece properly centred below its mark. This writing is not wasted effort; it is good practice in using your chosen equipment and in forming your letters well.

Use layout paper and rule writing lines for your chosen large-lettering size. Again, working with the widest generation first, write out all the names, remembering that you only have the space you marked off (in the example this was 4cm) for each name. Rule writing lines underneath each name for the smaller lettering size, then write in all the smaller information, trying to centralise it as well as possible. Do not worry if you judge poorly where to start and finish each line; this is one of the reasons for writing all the names in rough. As you progress, you get better at judging where each line of text should start. If you have spaced the lettering so off-centre that it encroaches too much on the next name in the row, then write it again using your failed attempt as a guide for the new one. If necessary, try a different arrangement of the notes for a person until they form a neat centred block beneath the name.

Now cut out and position each name centrally under its mark. The best method of fixing the names to the layout sheet is with masking tape. Cut a small piece about 3cm long and roll it back on itself, sticky side out. Apply it to the back of the cut-out name and position it on the chart. The process is fiddly, but masking tape will peel off and can be repositioned if necessary, so this gives a lot of flexibility in altering things later. If all has gone well and all the names fit, then proceed with the rest of the text in the same manner. If you have erred in your calculations, you may have to reposition the name marks or alter the lettering sizes.

better in this instance to arrange them in their family groups, equally spaced, where they will best tie in with the parents above (fig. 29).

This same situation might occur elsewhere in the chart, if you have a very small generation. Plot the larger generations to either side of the small one, then fit in the middle names at the most advantageous place. Fig. 30 shows a different set of information from the previous samples with a very small third generation. This row of names has been moved to the right to align better with the linking line to the parents in the second generation above.

(a)

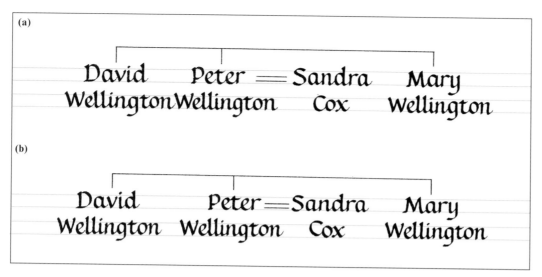

Fig. 31 Adjusting name markers

(b)

Sometimes a little fine adjustment is beneficial. This can be necessary if you have names of disparate lengths close together, as shown in fig. 31a. In this case it is better to move the markers slightly to give the longer names more breathing space (fig. 31b). The second name in the example is moved slightly to the right to give better spacing to the row.

Adding a title

A title for the work usually looks best centred at the top of the page in large bold letters. If you have been using nib sizes 4 and 5 or the equivalent for the main text, then a nib of about size 1° or lettering size 12-14mm in height will probably be appropriate for the title. The length of the title and the overall size of the chart might require smaller or larger lettering, so experiment with several sizes before you settle on the one you like best. As with the names, write the title in rough on layout paper, cut it out and attach it to the main layout sheet.

Charts which 'fizzle out' towards the top, often the case as the research becomes more difficult, sometimes benefit from having a title to one side (fig. 32). Offset titles are sometimes the only alternative, if you have a deep chart and have little room at the top of the sheet for the title. You can

peel off the names on the top few generations on the layout sheet and reposition them to make way for the offset title. If you prefer to keep to the centralised layout, you can restore the names to their

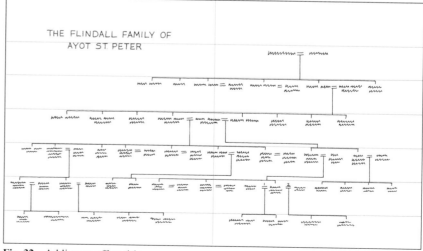

Fig. 32 Adding an offset title

original positions. Two or three lines of lettering usually look better for offset titles than one line. It is easy to pad out the length of a title with a few extra words – in the example-chart a simple title such as:

'The Flindall Family'

could be increased to

'The Flindall Family of Ayot St Peter'

or

'The Flindall Family of the County of Hertfordshire'.

Other possibilities are:

'The Descendants of Thomas Gurney Flindall of Hertfordshire'

or

'The Descendants of Thomas and Jane Flindall of Ayot St Peter'.

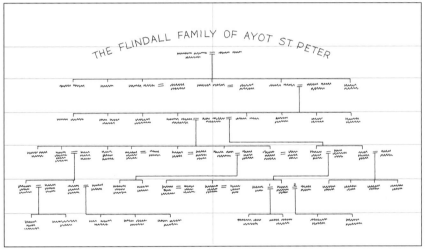

Fig. 33 Adding a curved title

You might want to base your title on a person nearer the bottom of the chart, describing it as:

'The Ancestors of Justin William Flindall'

Many people like to incorporate dates in a title such as:

'The Singleton Family from 1572-1990'

or

'The Pedigree of the Robertsons since 1780'

Some other simpler suggestions are:

'Winterbourne Family Tree'

'Lineage of the Winterbourne Family'

There are numerous possibilities and you should be able to arrive at something which is exactly the right size and description for your purposes.

An attractive method of adding a title is to curve the lettering across the top of the chart. It is not very difficult to write on curved lines provided that the curve is not too sharp and that the lines are very carefully drawn with an even curve. The safest way is with a curved template, but it is not always easy to find one that curves at exactly the right amount (fig. 33).

The title is usually the obvious part of a family tree to decorate if you want to give the chart a more attractive appearance. Various ways of embellishing titles are shown in chapter 4.

Keys

If you are using a lot of abbreviations which you want to explain, a small key in a convenient space is a good idea. This can save a lot of space and writing if you have long place names which are frequently repeated. Instead of writing Market Harborough repeatedly for a row of 10 children all baptised in the same town, you could simply write 'bap. M-H'. and explain more fully in the key.

A corner is usually the most convenient place for a key and it looks better boxed to separate it from the rest of the chart. Some readjustment to the overall layout might be necessary to accommodate your key, if the space is not readily available (fig. 34). As with the title, peel off and reposition the names on any area of the chart you think might work until you have found a suitable layout.

Final adjustments and margins

When all the text is fixed into position, take a good look at the whole chart and see if there is any way in which the layout could be improved. Perhaps the chart would look better with all the names in one generation placed slightly further apart. This is a fairly simple alteration to make. Peel off all the names in the row and fix them onto another sheet in the correct order. Rub out the original marks on the layout sheet and re-mark the line with the new distances apart for each name. The names can then be replaced on the layout sheet and correctly centred under their new marks.

A more difficult alteration is to the amount of space between each generation. Your chart may look unbalanced because one generation contains so little information that it leaves an unpleasant gap which would benefit from reduction. If you need to reduce the amount of space between generations, simply measure the amount to be discarded and cut it out of the page before joining the cut edges together again. Alternatively, you might have found that there was not enough space to fit in all the biographical details of one or two members of the family. To enlarge the space, cut the page at the relevant place and add an extra strip of paper. It is well worth taking the trouble to make these alterations, as they will give you the correct impression of the finished appearance of the chart. You should have this clearly decided before you begin on the final piece.

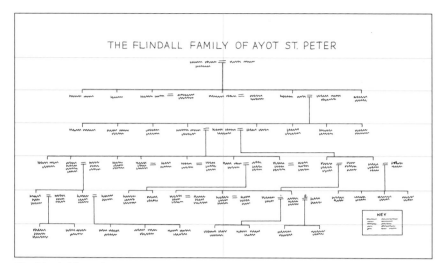

Fig. 34 Adding a key

Allow good margins around the work, so that it does not look cramped on the page and there will be room for the rebate of a frame or for trimming. Measure an equal distance on each side of the text for the left and right margins. The same distance will usually make a good top margin, but the bottom margin looks better if it is wider (fig. 35). Try a third or half as much again as the other margins, and then alter any of the margins as necessary to give the chart suitable surrounding space. Rule in all the lines so that you know exactly the size of the completed work.

Fig. 35 Margin widths – top and side margins equal, bottom margin slightly wider (shaded area represents extent of text).

Working on the real thing!

You are now ready to start work on the actual piece, using your chosen paper. You can either cut the sheet to the required size to start with or mark the dimensions on a larger sized page so that the work can be trimmed afterwards. The advantage of trimming later is that sometimes the edges of a page can become dog-eared or nicked slightly as you go through the various stages of measuring, writing etc. On the other hand, a very large sheet can be difficult to work on and so it is not helpful to make it too much larger than needed.

All the preliminary work on the layout can be carried out without the use of a guard sheet (see page 11) but once you come to the final work you should do your best to ensure that your hands touch the paper as little as possible. Use either a guard sheet fixed into position on your drawing board or make sure you always keep a guard sheet underneath your writing hand.

Measure off and draw the writing lines onto the paper with a fine pencil. An HB pencil is best as you will be able to rub out the lines easily afterwards. Be sure to measure and draw your lines very accurately as even small discrepancies in width make a lot of difference to the lettering and can make the text look very uneven.

Write from left to right and from the top of the page to the bottom to avoid resting your hand on wet lettering. Use your rough draft to ensure that you position each name correctly. Measure the length of each name or line of text on the draft and mark the writing lines with a pencil so that you know where to start and finish. It is difficult to be perfect with centred lettering as most people do not write every letter consistently, but, if you take care, the overall effect will be of good balance and clarity.

When all the text is complete, proofread it. It is very easy to make a mistake, especially with dates, when transferring data from one page to another. If you do find errors, these should not be too difficult to remove if you have chosen a good quality paper. Various methods for doing so are shown in the following chapter.

The connecting lines

Having satisfied yourself that the text is complete, the writing lines can be removed with a soft rubber. The connecting lines now need to be added. If you use paint for them, rather than the ink you used for the lettering, there are a few things to bear in mind. Some colours, especially red, tend to smudge if you rub over them, so be especially careful to remove all traces of the writing lines before you use the paint. Take care that there are no pencil marks remaining around the = signs as they are right on the writing lines. Winsor and Newton Designers Gouache is a good paint to use. It is available in tubes and is mixed with water to the required consistency. You want a fairly thin consistency but not so thin as to make the colour transparent. A touch of liquid gum arabic (available in small bottles from most

Fig. 36   A drop-line, four-generation chart

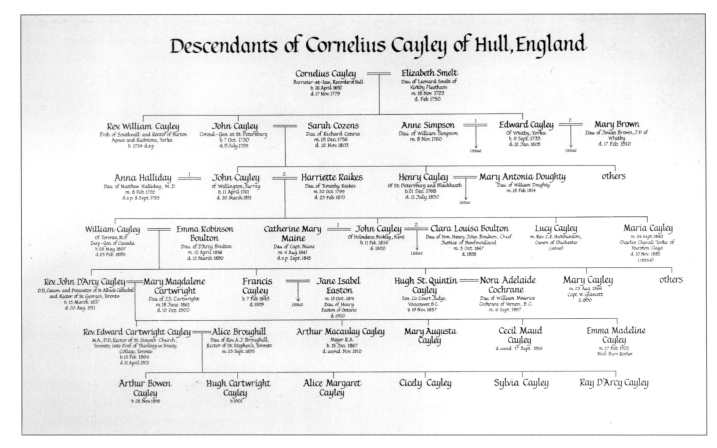

Descendants of Cornelius Cayley of Hull, England

Fig. 37 A family tree of seven generations.

art shops) can be mixed with colours with a tendency to smudge, and this will help to fix the pigment on the page. First try a little of the mixed paint on a piece of scrap paper to see what happens.

Practise ruling straight lines with your ruling pen or writing instrument to get used to handling the equipment. One of the worst things to happen when line ruling is for the ruler to slip, giving a line with a kink. Paint is a great deal more difficult than ink to remove from a page, so proceed with caution. Rule in all the horizontal lines first; when you are sure the paint is completely dry, turn the page round and rule in the verticals. It only remains to trim the page and the chart is ready for framing.

Fig. 36 shows a simple drop-line chart of four generations. Fig. 37 shows a seven-generation chart with the number of people on each row evenly distributed to either side of centre.

The Birth Brief

A much easier form of pedigree to lay out is the 'birth brief'. This type of chart begins with one person, the main subject of the pedigree, and goes back through each generation naming the parents of each person each time, but showing no other relatives. Printed forms (fig. 38) are available for you to fill in with your own family details. The forms usually run from left to right, and it is a simple matter to transform this information into a vertical drop-line chart. A drop-line pedigree will give you a pyramid-shaped chart, as the number of persons doubles with each generation further back. The sample shown in fig. 39 goes back four generations to the great grandparents of the main subject.

The layout of this type of chart is very simple. If you want to make an attractive wall hanging of this information, it is nonetheless worth making an initial

	PARENTS	GRANDPARENTS	GREAT GRANDPARENTS	GREAT GREAT GRANDPARENTS

Birth Brief Of

Name
Born/Bapt.
at

Occupation etc

Married
at
Spouse
Born
at

Parents column:

Father
Born/Bapt.
at

Occupation etc

Died/Bur.
at

Mother
Born/Bapt.
at

Married
at

Died/Bur.
at

Grandparents column:

Father
Born/Bapt.
at

Occupation etc

Died/Bur.
at

Mother
Born/Bapt.
at

Married
at

Died/Bur.
at

Father
Born/Bapt.
at

Occupation etc

Died/Bur.
at

Mother
Born/Bapt.
at

Married
at

Died/Bur.
at

Great Grandparents column:

Father
Born/Bapt.
at
Occupation
Died/Bur.
at

Mother
Born/Bapt.
at
Married
at
Died/Bur.
at

Father
Born/Bapt.
at
Occupation
Died/Bur.
at

Mother
Born/Bapt.
at
Married
at
Died/Bur.
at

Father
Born/Bapt.
at
Occupation
Died/Bur.
at

Mother
Born/Bapt.
at
Married
at
Died/Bur.
at

Father
Born/Bapt.
at
Occupation
Died/Bur.
at

Mother
Born/Bapt.
at
Married
at
Died/Bur.
at

Great Great Grandparents column:

Father
Born/Bapt.   at
Died/Bur.   at
Mother
Born/Bapt.   at
Married   at
Died/Bur.   at
Father
Born/Bapt.   at
Died/Bur.   at
Mother
Born/Bapt.   at
Married   at
Died/Bur.   at
Father
Born/Bapt.   at
Died/Bur.   at
Mother
Born/Bapt.   at
Married   at
Died/Bur.   at
Father
Born/Bapt.   at
Died/Bur.   at
Mother
Born/Bapt.   at
Married   at
Died/Bur.   at
Father
Born/Bapt.   at
Died/Bur.   at
Mother
Born/Bapt.   at
Married   at
Died/Bur.   at
Father
Born/Bapt.   at
Died/Bur.   at
Mother
Born/Bapt.   at
Married   at
Died/Bur.   at
Father
Born/Bapt.   at
Died/Bur.   at
Mother
Born/Bapt.   at
Married   at
Died/Bur.   at
Father
Born/Bapt.   at
Died/Bur.   at
Mother
Born/Bapt.   at
Married   at
Died/Bur.   at

Fig. 38   Printed birth brief

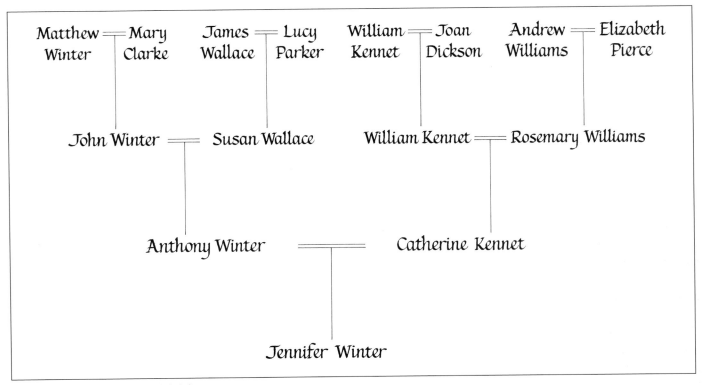

Fig. 39   Vertically arranged birth brief

draft of the whole chart, to see exactly how to space all the information for a neat and pleasing effect. It also makes a good exercise in the whole process of producing a family tree, so is worth doing as a preliminary to a larger more complex chart.

Start with the top generation, which is the widest, and, when you have found the right combination of lettering sizes for the work, rule a set of writing lines about five to six centimetres from the top of a large sheet of layout paper. Write out the top row of names in a line leaving an even amount of space between each name. As this generation will be much wider than the others, it is best to write any second names and the surname on lines below the forename so that the width is kept to a minimum. You will need to allow enough space between each couple for the = signs. Having allowed for a margin to the side of each of the end names of the row, you can now calculate the width of your chart. Write in the smaller details under each person, doing your best to centralise the information line by line.

Measure and rule in writing lines for the next generation down. Leave a reasonable amount of space between the two generations. Pencil in the = signs for each couple, then take down a line from each to stop just short of the new lines (fig. 40).

You will need to write the second row so that the names come out under the vertical lines. To ensure accuracy write the next row on a separate sheet of layout paper. Cut out each name and stick it onto the first master copy in the correct position. If you feel confident of being accurate you can write directly onto the

same sheet. If you write the new names on a separate sheet, you can match up the writing lines on both sheets to make sure you position the names correctly. When the entire second row is in place draw in the = signs between each couple, draw a new set of writing lines for the third generation and proceed as for the second.

The names on the second and third line can be written with both forename and surname on the same line, as they need to stretch a little wider across the page to make contact with the lines descending from the parents. It might sometimes be necessary to bring the lines across horizontally so that they fall in the right places. Finally the bottom name is centred on the page. If your bottom two lines do not fall in the centre, because of the discrepancy in lengths of names at the top of the chart, it is an easy matter to adjust the positioning of the last two generations to balance up the chart.

When you have the whole spread of the text in front of you, adjustments can be made, if necessary, to improve the layout. You might decide that a little more space between the generations would improve the overall look. If a title is required, a straightforward centred line of large lettering will probably be best. When the whole layout is complete you can proceed through the stages to production of the finished work as previously described.

Fig. 41 shows a completed birth-brief-type chart with plenty of biographical detail under each person.

If you want to draw up a birth brief keeping to the 'left to right' type of layout used on the printed sheets, then follow the instructions for the production of this sort of chart in chapter 6.

Matthew = Mary   James = Lucy   William = Joan   Andrew = Elizabeth
Winter   Clarke Wallace Parker Kennet   Dickson Williams Pierce

Fig. 40 Plotting the first generation of a birth brief

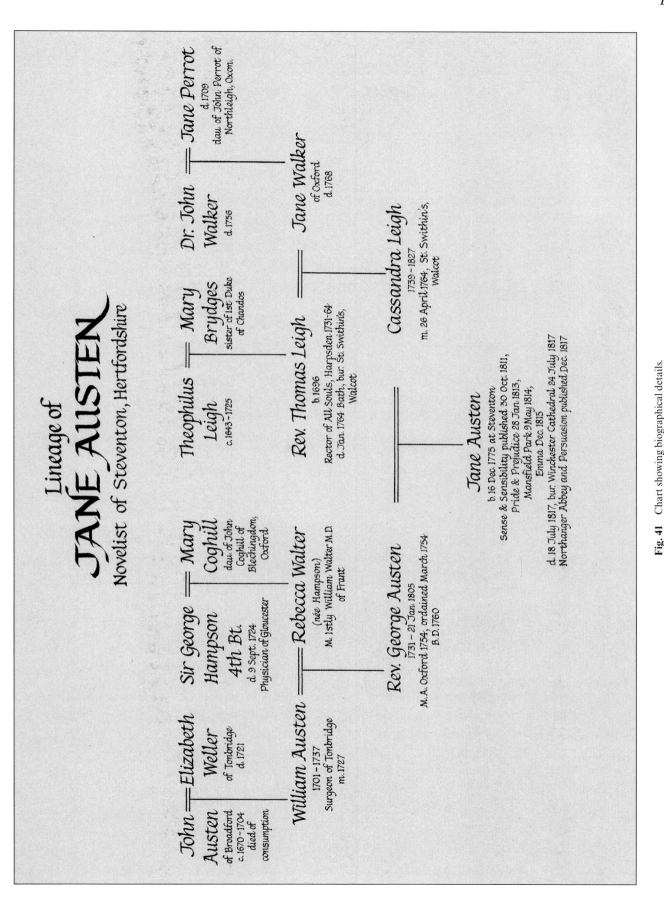

Lineage of JANE AUSTEN

Novelist of Steventon, Hertfordshire

John Austen ═ Elizabeth Weller
of Broadford
c.1670-1704
died of
consumption
of Tonbridge
d.1721

Sir George Hampson ═ Mary Coghill
4th Bt.
d.9 Sept.1724
Physician of Gloucester
dau. of John Coghill of Bledchingdom, Oxford

Theophilus Leigh ═ Mary Brydges
c.1643-1725
sister of 1st Duke of Chandos

Dr. John Walker ═ Jane Perrot
d.1756
d.1709
dau. of John Perrot of Northleigh, Oxon.

William Austen ═ Rebecca Walter
1701-1737
Surgeon of Tonbridge
m.1727
(née Hampson)
M.1stly William Walter M.D. of Frant

Rev. Thomas Leigh ═ Jane Walker
b.1696
Rector of All Souls, Harpsden.1731-64
d.Jan.1764 Bath, bur. St. Swithin's, Walcot
of Oxford
d.1768

Rev. George Austen ═ Cassandra Leigh
1731 – 21 Jan.1805
M.A. Oxford.1754, ordained March.1754
B.D.1760
1739 – 1827
m. 26 April.1764, St. Swithin's, Walcot

Jane Austen
b.16 Dec.1775 at Steventon
Sense & Sensibility published 30 Oct. 1811,
Pride & Prejudice 28 Jan.1813,
Mansfield Park 9 May 1814,
Emma Dec. 1815
d. 18 July 1817, bur. Winchester Cathedral 24 July 1817
Northanger Abbey and Persuasion published Dec. 1817

Fig. 41 Chart showing biographical details.

Chapter 3
Problem Solving

There are very few people lucky enough to have a chart which fits together with no problem areas. The larger you choose to make the chart the more likely you are to introduce difficult relationships. Some suggested ways of overcoming these are shown below.

Re-marriage

The best method of including a second husband or wife is to place the two spouses on either side of the subject, as shown in fig. 42. It is a good idea to number the marriages above the == signs so that it is clear at a glance in which order the marriages occurred. The advantage of this method is that children from both marriages can be shown without confusion about which parents produced each child.

Another often used method is to line up the spouses underneath the subject (fig. 43). This method is fine where there are no children and it saves a lot of space. Subsequent marriages can be added with no difficulty. The disadvantage, if there are children of either marriage and these are to be shown, is that you must indicate which spouse produced which child. Dates of marriage and birth will usually make this apparent, but not always, and it detracts from the straightforward clarity of the chart. Sometimes, however, if space is short, it is the best way of making good use of what you have.

If a third marriage needs to be included the arrangement shown in fig. 44 is probably the best. Once again this method shows the children from each marriage with clarity. The order in which the marriages are arranged is often dictated by the children to be included. It is an advantage if they can appear in descending order of age from left to right

Mary Green ══ James Wilson ══ Jane White

Fig. 42 Arranging order of names to include a second marriage

James Wilson
1 ══ Mary Green
2 ══ Jane White

Fig. 43 Alternative arrangement if there are no children

Mary Green ══ James Wilson ══ Susan Robinson
══ Jane White

Fig. 44 Arranging order of three spouses

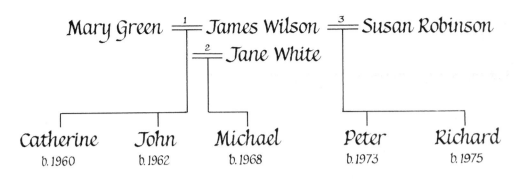

Fig. 45 Keeping children of multiple marriages in chronological order

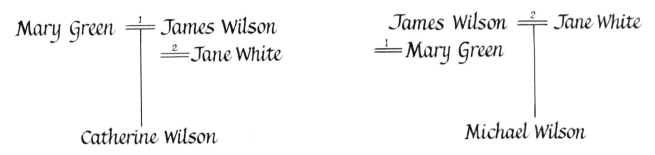

Fig. 46 (a) Offspring from first marriage only; (b) Offspring from second marriage only

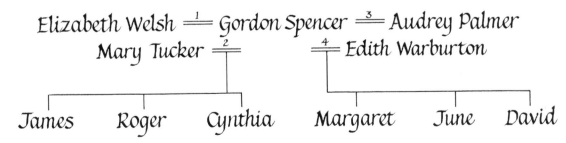

Fig. 47 Alternative layout for three spouses

Fig. 48 Arranging multiple marriages so that children can be added in correct sequence

on the following generation, as shown in fig. 45.

A combination of the two methods above can be used if there are no children from one of the marriages (figs. 46a and b). Sometimes the method of lining up the spouses, from left to right after the subject, is used for showing several marriages (fig. 47). This has the advantages of showing each spouse in the correct order and the children can appear in order of birth, but I tend not to use it as it appears, at first glance, as if two women (in the example) are shown linked by marriage lines.

Fourth marriages occasionally occur. If you are unlucky enough to have this problem, the main thing to remember is that, if any marriage has produced children to be shown on the chart, then the names should be arranged so that the fruitful marriages can have uninterrupted lines from parents to offspring and, if possible, the marriages should be arranged so that the children appear in correct order of birth (fig. 48). Remember in all cases that sufficient room must be allowed for the biographical detail you wish to include with each person. If, in the example shown in fig.48, a large amount of biographical detail were to be included for the husband or either of the top two wives, then the names of the underneath two wives would have to be dropped down considerably and this might necessitate placing the generations further apart to accommodate all the text.

Natural children

Various methods have been used to show an unmarried partner and natural children. The method most successful for the layout is a connection with wavy or zigzag lines down to the offspring (fig. 49). Obviously, if it is not desirable to make the illegitimate connection too obvious, the zigzag line need not be used and a less conspicuous 'natural son/daughter' can be included in the biographical details.

Adopted children are sometimes shown in a similar manner. It is up to the individual draftsman to decide what is required. The aim is obviously to indicate that the relationship is not that of all the others shown on the chart and the method chosen simply needs to show this in a suitable manner.

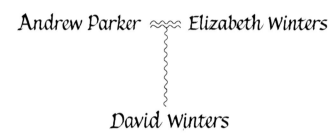

Fig. 49 Wavy lines for natural children

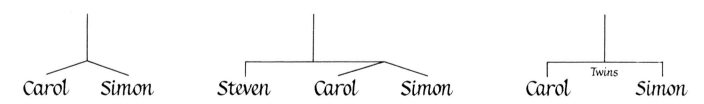

Fig. 50 Linking twins

Twins

Twins can simply be shown as individual children in order of time of birth but some people like to emphasise the connection by linking the twins together in some way and various methods are shown in fig. 50.

Intermarriage

Marriages between different branches of the family occur very frequently and can cause numerous problems. Often the simplest solution is to write in the relevant people twice and cross reference the names, but this does not make the relationship very apparent.

It is usually necessary for connecting lines to cross other lines when linking marriages between relatives. To make it clear which line leads to which family,

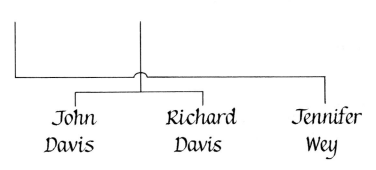

interrupt one of the lines with a little bridging curve, as shown in fig. 51. On very complex charts many such bridges will be needed, but it is fairly easy to follow each line to its destination.

It is often necessary to place children out of chronological order when joining marriages between relatives or when adding large new families through a marriage. You have the choice either of keeping the order chronological but forsaking an easy-to-follow layout, or of

Fig. 51 Bridging overlapping connecting lines

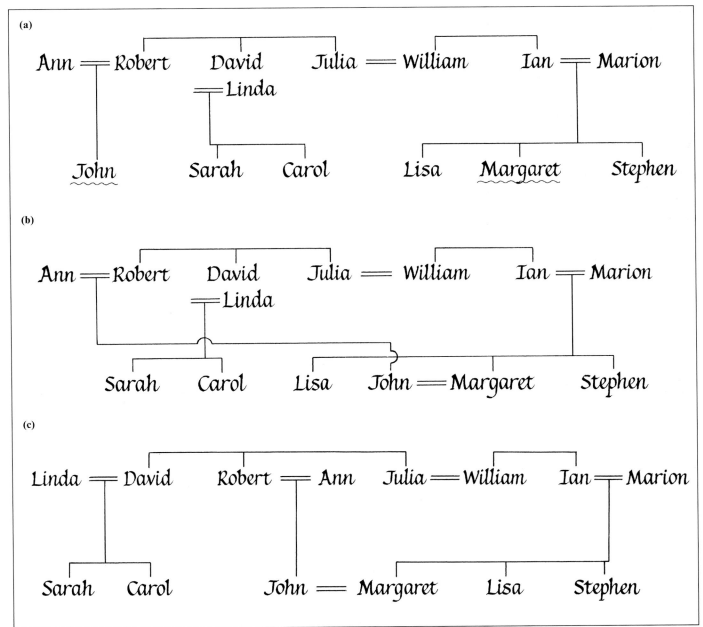

Fig. 52 (a) If John and Margaret marry how can they be linked together? (b) A solution using two bridges (c) An alternative solution avoiding bridges

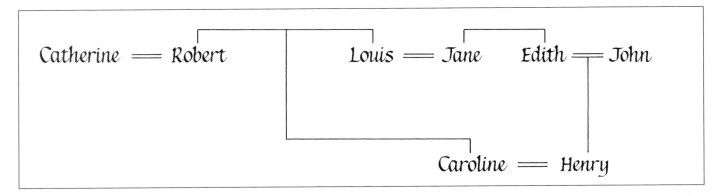

placing the siblings out of chronological sequence. I prefer to abandon chronological sequence, as it is easy to pick out from the dates of birth the age sequence of a family. If people are shown twice on a chart or cross referenced to another area then it is much more difficult to track each line of descent.

Take, for example, the information in fig. 52a. If the couple underlined marry, then to link them poses a problem. In fig. 52b John is moved across to his partner by running his connecting line over the intervening lines. Alternatively, if the order of the names of the families in the parent generation is altered, the couple can be brought side by side without the use of any bridges (fig. 52c). Obviously, if Julia and William produce a family, the situation changes and bridges will almost certainly be required. It is up to you to decide which arrangement best solves your layout problems.

Marriages between generations on different levels cause difficulties. It is best to bring the spouse from the generation above down to the lower level as children of the marriage will fit better with the following generation. This can spoil the normal set-up for relationships, with nephews and nieces appearing as grandnephews and nieces, but as the

Fig. 53
Linking marriages between different generations

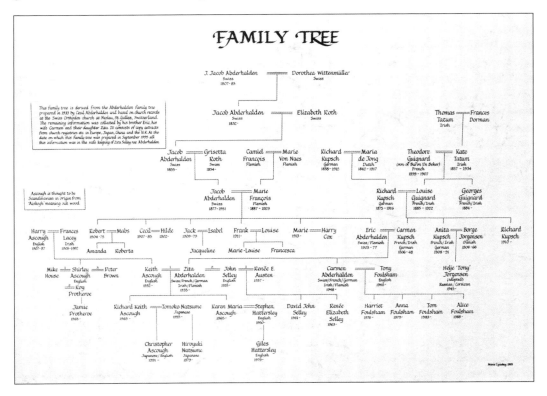

Fig. 54 Fitting 'trapped' branches between the main generations

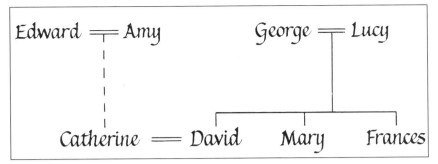

Fig. 55 Dotted lines for doubtful information

relationships are different depending on which branch of the family is considered, there is little alternative. Fig. 53 shows an example of this arrangement.

If descent lines are trapped by children and marriages, providing there are no offspring for the trapped persons, the bridges can be avoided by inserting the relevant people into the space between the

Fig. 56 Overcoming various problems

generations, as shown in fig. 54. In the example this method is a better and clearer option than taking each of the trapped families to either side on long connecting lines with bridges over the trapping lines.

Doubtful connections

Much research contains hazy areas where information has been obtained which is likely to be part of the family history but no absolute proof is available. If much hard work has gone into finding the information, researchers can be very reluctant to omit it from the chart. The best thing to do is to include the information, but to use broken connecting lines as shown in fig. 55. The situation can be fully explained in the biographical notes underneath each person or in the key.

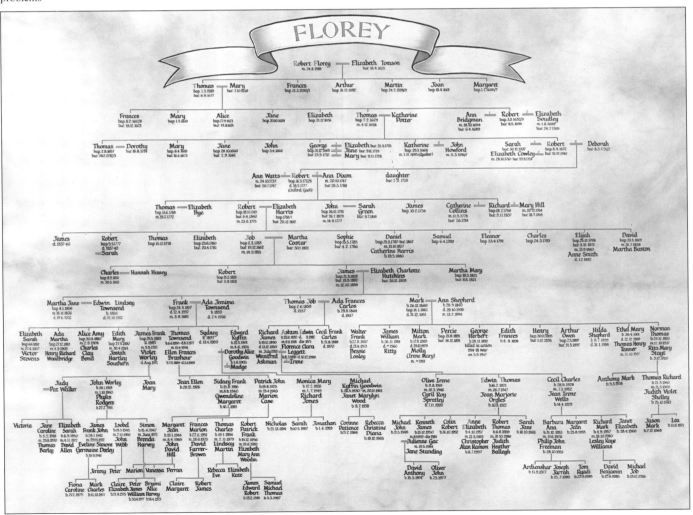

Fig. 56 shows a large chart on vellum which illustrates many ways in which different problems were overcome. The third generation from the top shows two different methods of showing three marriages to the same person. One entry shows all three spouses lined up one below the next. This was possible as no children were to be shown. The second entry with three marriages, further along the line, shows the third marriage set to the right to enable the connecting line to pass down and below the other information to the following generation.

The tenth generation down shows an area where various second marriages caused much congestion. It was necessary, because of the large overall width of the generation, to place both marriages beneath the main subject. The connecting lines to the children had to be positioned so that they could drop down from the relevant = sign.

The bottom generation shows how children had to be stepped on two different levels to avoid excessive width. Each chart creates its unique set of problems.

Space saving methods

Very often you simply cannot give as much space as you would like to certain people or areas on large charts. Sometimes the overall width would be otherwise so great that you would not have large enough paper or perhaps the space available for hanging the finished piece will determine the extent of your chart. Often the layout calls for cramped spacing in places so that the overall effect will be balanced. The methods shown below are compromises through necessity and at the sacrifice of clarity, but all too often they have to be employed for the sake of including all the required information without producing a chart of excessive proportions.

Large families of children can be treated in a similar manner to multiple marriages, by listing the children one below the other, as shown in fig. 57. This method was used frequently on older pedigrees, particularly for listing large

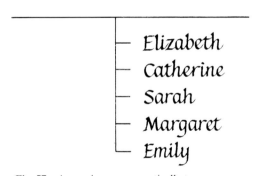

Fig. 57 Arranging names vertically to save space

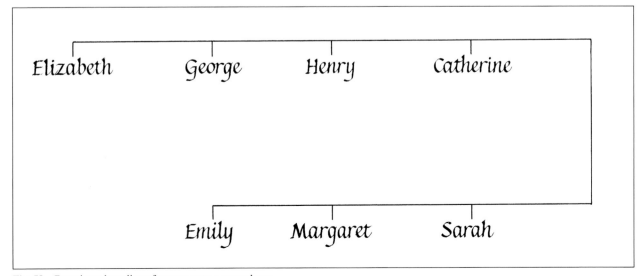

Fig. 58 Running a long line of names onto a second row

families of daughters. It was often unnecessary to show any further details for the females and so this method presented a solution to the space problem. If any child proved worthy of more detail, he or she had to be placed on a separate mark so that, if required, room was available for biographical details and connection to a spouse.

Long generations which cannot be fitted onto a chart without spoiling the overall balance can be wrapped over and carried to a line further down the page (fig. 58). As you can see, this method raises a multitude of problems, if you wish to continue the line from any of the entries in the top line, but sometimes it can be a satisfactory solution. When the names reach the second line continue the order in line sequence so that the youngest appears on the left end of the underneath line.

Offsetting members of a generation is sometimes necessary to enable all the names to be included without producing too wide a chart. Fig. 59 shows an example.

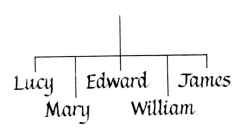

Fig. 59   Offsetting names to save space

Removing Errors

However careful you try to be, mistakes occur. Take out an error with a very hard white rubber. Typewriter rubbers are perfect for this and you can be very accurate with them, confining your erasure to a small area. Buy one with a little brush on the end if you can, as this is very useful for removing the rubbings. Proceed with caution to avoid rubbing a hole in the paper. It is a good idea to experiment first with a spare scrap of the paper you are using. Write a word and try to remove it so that you can see how hard you can rub without spoiling the paper. You do not want to disturb the paper surface more than is absolutely necessary as it has to be in a good enough condition afterwards to be written over again. When all the incorrect writing is removed, smooth the paper surface with a hard smooth object so that all the disturbed fibres are compressed again. The correct item to use is called a bone folder, a long thin smooth piece of bone which will not mark the surface. Bone folders can be bought from good art shops. If you cannot find one, try some other smooth hard object. I have used the back of a spoon successfully for this job, but ensure that the object you use will not transfer any colour to the page. Take care not to press too hard; some papers become shiny if you rub them hard and others actually show the dented area.

Lightly rule in again your guide lines and write the new letters with extreme caution. Some papers do not take kindly to this treatment and you might find that the ink now spreads out like blotting paper; this is why it is best to experiment first with the paper you intend to use for the work. You can rub a little powder called gum sandarac (available from art shops) into the damaged area, which should prevent the ink from spreading.

Another method of removing errors is by using a scalpel to scrape away the letters. This only really works satisfactorily on thick papers and over small areas, but, if you use a delicate touch and work gradually, the damage to the paper surface can sometimes be less traumatic than by the use of a hard rubber. Another point to bear in mind when choosing a paper is that some of the very decorative papers now available actually have a coating which you will wear away if you need to correct errors. This can leave a white patch underneath which you will somehow have to cover up.

Updating

If you are fairly sure that you will want to add more to your chart, then you can leave space accordingly. Gaps in the main body of the text need to be carefully judged. You often have to leave more space than you will eventually need, to allow for the maximum text you are likely to add.

Space can also be left at the bottom of the chart for additional children and for future generations. This is a sensible option, if you do not intend to frame the chart, and there is no harm in having a large blank area at the bottom. Charts to be framed look less attractive with large blank areas, so you must decide how much blank space you are prepared to put up with for the sake of possible future additions.

Continuation charts

Another method of updating your family history is to make a separate chart cross-referenced to the original. You may be able to find room to insert a continuation marker on the main chart as shown in fig. 60. This method is also useful if you have a very complicated chart or a very large one which is almost impossible to fit on

Fig. 60   Continuation marker

one sheet. Different branches of the family can be shown on different charts which are cross-referenced to each other with relevant symbols. Some examples are shown in fig. 61.

When you are updating an existing chart it is important to match the lettering sizes and styles as accurately as possible. Old charts frequently use a style known as copperplate (fig. 62). This can be very difficult to write and needs a high degree of accuracy because the letters are so narrow and slope at a pronounced angle.

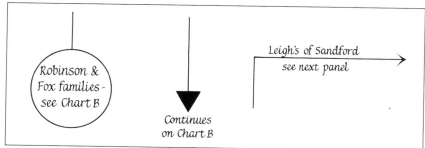

Fig. 61   Cross-referencing symbols

To overcome this problem, write the lettering with a pencil first and then go over it with the pen and ink. When the ink has dried, rub out any of the visible guidelines. This method can be used with any lettering style which proves difficult to copy. You will need to study the existing alphabet carefully to see how each of the letters is formed. Measure the height of the letters and the width of the nib of the pen used. Sometimes old charts were not very accurately drawn so that you get a mixture of uneven line widths. It is worth taking a little trouble to achieve a good match, as the document will not look so attractive if the new section is glaringly different.

Fig. 62   Copperplate lettering

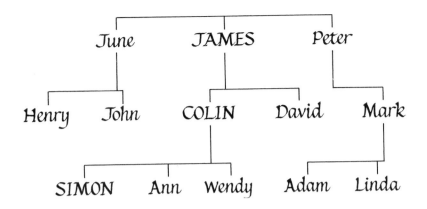

Fig. 63 Using capitals to emphasise a line of descent

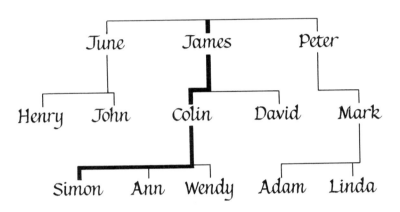

Fig. 64 Using a thicker line to emphasise a line of descent

Fig. 65 Take care when working on circled areas

Emphasising lines of descent

From a large chart containing many people it can be difficult to pick out a particular line of descent. If there is one line that, for one reason or another, you wish to emphasise, perhaps the descent of an estate through various generations or the eldest male line, or the junior branch of a large family which leads to your own particular branch, this can be done in various ways.

Firstly, the names themselves can be written in a different colour or a different lettering style (Italic, capitals etc.) from the rest of the people, as in fig. 63.

Secondly, the lines can be thickened as in fig. 64. Extra care must be taken when using the ruling pen. The points of the pen can either be widened for a thicker line or the normal width can be used but in several thicknesses. This is perhaps preferable as you can continue adding strokes until you are satisfied with the width attained. Practise the effect you want to achieve on layout paper first; thicker lines can make connection problems with other lines. Take care when you come to corners such as the circled areas in fig. 65.

Thirdly a series of different coloured lines can be used to indicate different families on the chart. The rule to follow with this method is that, where one family meets another, make the = sign the colour of the husband's family and the following children his colour. This adds considerably to the overall appearance of the chart, but make sure to plot carefully on your rough draft before you start which line will be which colour. It is good to reserve black for any part of the chart which does not conform to the main lines you are identifying with the colours, fig. 66.

There are ways of overcoming every problem on a family tree chart, and with a little thought and careful planning the general clarity of the chart can be much improved.

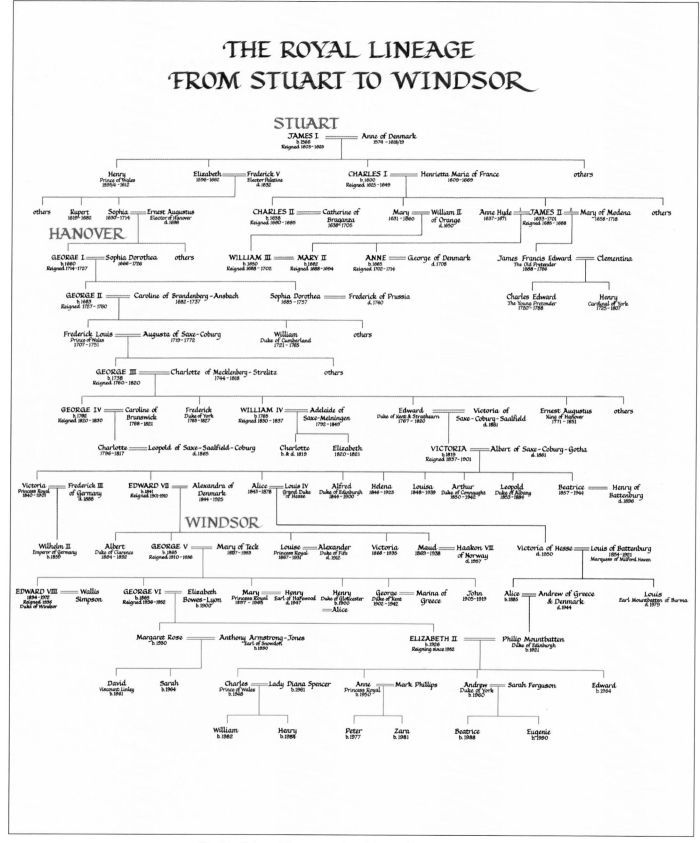

Fig. 66 Coloured lines are used to pick out different family groups

Chapter 4
Illustrations & Decoration

A large sheet of lettering can benefit greatly from some form of decoration. There are various ways of adding decorative material to a family tree chart.

Title decoration

The simplest method is to elaborate the title. This can be done with coloured lettering or the letters can be enlarged and attractive detail can be added to the centres or to the surrounds. Adapting the title to fit a scroll shape can be very effective, giving the appearance of a banner across the top of the chart.

Coloured lettering – if you decide to write with coloured ink or paint, the same considerations apply as were important when using paint for connecting lines. A good quality ink or paint, which will not fade, smudge, or flow too rapidly from the pen, should be used. In addition to the title, you could try writing all the initial letters of the names in colour which will give touches of colour throughout the chart and add interest to the document.

Brush lettering – apart from pen-written letters, large title letters can be written with a paintbrush, which will give you much more scope for decoration. Very fine-pointed good quality brushes should be used to produce accurate letters. Sable brushes from art shops and stationers are best and the smallest sizes, 0 and 1, will be the most useful. When you buy a fine tipped brush look carefully at the tip to see if the hairs are in good condition, and check that they are not bent over or splayed apart. The hairs need to meet in a neat point when the brush is wet. A fine point to the brush will make all the difference to the quality of your letters and

also to the accuracy and detail you can put into illustrations. Water-based paints are best for this sort of work as many inks rot the hairs on a brush very quickly and spoil your ability to produce fine lines. Mixing palettes will be needed for each colour, and it is a good idea to choose something with a lid to keep the mixed colour fresh over several days. Tubes of silver and gold paint are available in the designer's gouache range of colours and these can be very useful for a little highlighting here and there. Buy a few cheap larger brushes for mixing colours— you will spoil your fine brushes if you mix paint with them.

One of the best alphabets for titles is the Versal alphabet illustrated in fig. 67. The letters in the example are shown in outline form so that the construction can be easily seen, but the letters can be one solid colour, outlined or patterned. Versals can be written either with a brush or pen. For pen-written letters the outline is made by using a small nib such as a size 4 or 5 William Mitchell nib, and then the outline is filled in either with the nib itself or with a small brush. For brush-painted letters the whole letter is produced with a small fine brush. The basic letter shapes can be made more elaborate by elongating the tails of letters such as A and R. This can look particularly effective if the decorative letters come at the beginning or end of a whole title in Versals.

Begin by roughly sketching the title words in pencil onto the draft copy, in letters of the size you think will work best. Next, rule a set of writing lines on a separate piece of layout paper at the distance apart you have made the rough lettering and write the letters with your chosen instrument, taking care to size and space them well. You can then cut out the strip of trial lettering and position it correctly on the chart; if the nib size has not produced the correct size of letter, you can try again with another size. When you come to write the title on the chart, use the draft to measure exactly where the writing lines should be placed and rule them onto the actual piece (this is usually done when all of the main text has been completed). The letters can then be written in complete confidence that they are in the right size and position on the chart.

If you are using brush lettering, draw the letters carefully with a pencil on layout paper, then cut out the strip of lettering and position it correctly on the actual chart. Use tracing paper or transfer paper to trace the letters onto the work. Red transfer paper, which is thin paper coated with a reddish brown powder, is very useful for transferring any sort of illustration onto the chart. It is available from specialist art suppliers and is preferable to tracing paper as it eliminates the laborious process of tracing onto the back of your drawing then tracing down from the front again onto the work. A slight disadvantage is that new sheets can have a lot of surplus red pigment on the surface which will get onto your chart. Although it can be removed with a rubber, to avoid the problem first wipe the transfer paper with a tissue, so that most of the excess powder is removed. When the traced outlines of your letters are in place, paint in the centres first, then the outlines. It is a good idea to put in first all the vertical outlines then turn the paper sideways and make all the horizontal outlines. This will keep all the horizontals

Fig. 67 Versal letters

in line. Turn the paper again to make the diagonals and finish the letters by putting in the curved lines as accurately as possible. A good effect can be produced by making the outlines a different colour from the centres of the letters.

A simple and effective method of embellishing the title is to use enlarged Versals for the initial letters of each word as shown in fig. 68. Make the initial letter start slightly below the bottom writing line, and finish at about double the height of normal writing lines (see guide lines in fig. 68). This looks more attractive than a large letter standing on the same level as the smaller text. A considerable degree of embellishment can be added to a versal letter and a few possibilities are shown in fig. 69. Some letters lend themselves to decoration better than others, but with a little imagination they can all be made to look very attractive. Floral or filigree decoration around the letters looks very good (fig. 70). The examples shown were drawn first with a pencil, then painted carefully with a fine brush, but a narrow pen could also have been used and some people might find this method easier than using a tiny brush. Always try to start floral decoration by making the stems grow out of the letters, then follow on by producing leaves, flowers and seeds in the natural direction that they would grow on the plant. The stems can be twisted and turned to fit and flowers and leaves can be added wherever there is a suitable space. Filigree decoration is built up in progressive layers outwards from the letter. It is important not to obscure the actual letter so that it is difficult to tell which it is. Be especially careful with letters which can easily be mistaken for others, such as E and F or P and R, where one tiny line in the wrong place can make the letter appear to be a different one. A whole title in versal letters is shown in fig. 71.

There are stencils available for making large lettering and this is a good option if you find versals difficult to produce. The letters in fig. 72 were made

Fig. 68 Versal initial letters

Fig. 69 Decorated versal initials

Fig. 70 Floral and filigree decoration on Versal capital letters

Fig. 71 Title in Versal letters

39

with a fairly cheap plastic stencil purchased from a stationer. Draw the first letter you need, then rule in writing lines for the rest of the letters so that they will appear in a straight line. Once you have the outlines in place just follow the same steps described above for brush-painted letters.

Simply underlining the title and finishing off the ends with arrow heads or small motifs (as shown in fig. 73) can improve the overall appearance of the chart. Use a ruling pen or ruling compass if your title is curved.

When an initial letter contains decoration which represents something or tells a story, it is known as an historiated initial. This type of illustration was used a great deal on old manuscripts, often in a whole series of pictures throughout a document relating the historical progress of a group of people. The initial letter of a title is again the obvious choice for this sort of treatment. Sometimes people wish to include stories of particularly colourful characters in the family's history so a special paragraph can be designed and illustrated then placed in a suitable gap on the chart. Make sure to cross reference this information with the actual person on the main part of the chart. The size and detail used for historiated initials must be carefully chosen to blend with the rest of the chart (fig. 74). The illustrations should be neither too big and overpowering nor

ABCDEFG RICHARDS FAMILY

Fig. 72   Stencilled capital letters

Fig. 73   Underlining a title

Fig. 74   Historiated initials

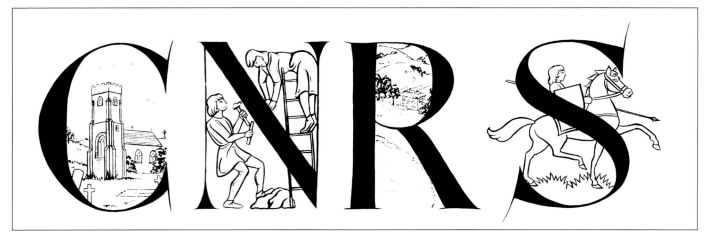

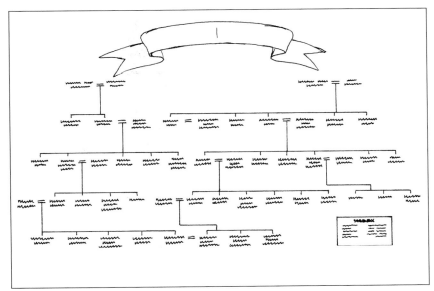

Fig. 75 Sketching the position of a scroll title

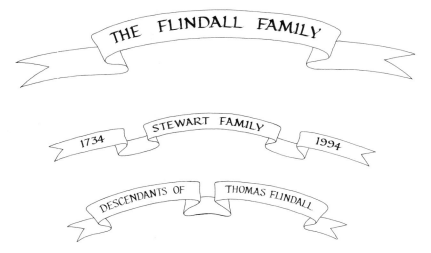

Fig. 76 Adapting a scroll to fit the title

you mark the centre of the chart with a vertical line before sketching in the scroll shape you would like to use, so that it is symmetrical. You do not need to be too accurate at this stage—you are simply trying to establish the size of scroll you want and the general shape. Sketch the lettering on to the scroll shape so that you can see if the arrangement of twists and turns in the scroll will suit the number of words you need to include. You can adapt scrolls to take the amount of lettering you have, as shown in fig. 76.

When you have an arrangement of scroll and lettering which works out well, draw half the scroll as accurately as you can on layout paper. Measure the width of the scroll at different points so that it is the same width from beginning to end. Now, using a sheet of tracing paper, trace over the first half then flip this over and trace down the other side so that the ends join. This will ensure that your scroll will be completely symmetrical. You can usually tell at this stage if you have made any errors in the drawing of the curves, as a mirror image often shows up discrepancies.

Measure guidelines carefully with a ruler as shown in fig. 77a, making a series of points at equal distances to form the writing lines for the lettering. Count up the number of letters in the title and also add one for each space between words to make the total width of letter spaces required for the title. Mark the central letter or gap so that this can be made to correspond with the centre point of your scroll. Write the second half of the lettering which can be used to judge where to start the first half, fig. 77b. This method saves a lot of otherwise wasted time. If you start from the beginning of the title and try to guess how long it will be, you will probably find that the whole title, when completed, is not centred properly and needs to be re-drawn.

When all the lettering is roughly in place, experiment with nib, pen or stencil sizes to find one which will produce

so small that they are lost and insignificant. Scenes containing buildings of relevance to the family, or illustrations of trades connected with certain members, or famous exploits make good subjects for this type of illustration.

Scrolls – scroll-shaped titles work very well as the decoration is evenly dispersed across the top of the chart rather than being heavier towards one corner, as with a historiated initial. To determine the size of scroll, begin by making a very rough sketch of the shape and position you want, as shown in fig. 75. It is easier if

correctly proportioned letters. It is a good idea to write out the whole title in rough to make sure that it will fit properly. If the letters are to be painted, they can be drawn carefully on draft paper ready for transferring to the work. When you are ready to add the title to the chart, trace the scroll from the layout sheet onto the main chart.

Paint on a base coat if required. Do not use a base coat if you are writing rather than painting the lettering; writing onto painted paper is not very successful, as the painted surface is very porous and your letters will not be sharp. The painted base coat should be a pale colour using a consistency of paint which is neither so thin as to be transparent nor so thick that it produces ridges as it dries. Try to make the base layer as even as possible. Next, outline the scroll with a darker colour, fig. 78. If you are writing the letters with a pen, carefully measure and draw in the writing lines before writing the lettering. If you have the patience, the scroll can be carefully modelled with darker shades of the base coat to give a more realistic appearance. Work in progressive stages through about three shades as shown in fig. 79. Even if you have not used a base coat, it is still good to work some detail into the curves. Scrolls look smart in a cream colour with dark brown edges. It looks very attractive to make the reverse side of the ribbon a different colour, such as red. When this stage is completed, brush-painted lettering can be traced onto the scroll and then painted in very carefully with a fine brush.

Borders

A border around the whole chart is another attractive means of decorating the work. The border can be anything from a simple narrow strip to a wide panel of illustrations. The border can be used all around the work or on just one or two of the sides (fig. 80). You can use a border to alter the proportions of the whole chart. For example, a long narrow chart would

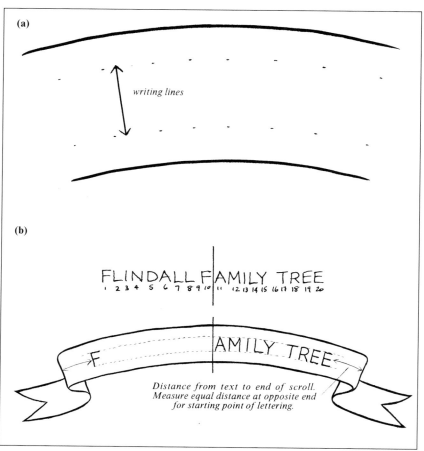

Fig. 77   (a) Measuring writing lines for curved lettering; (b) Centralising the scroll lettering

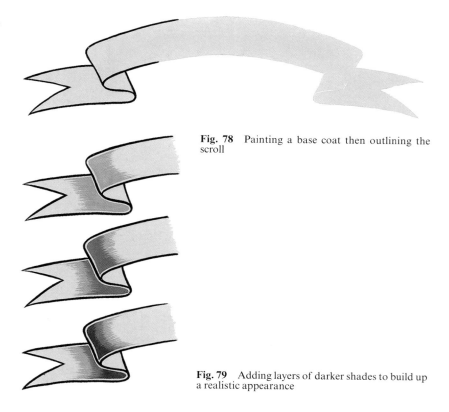

Fig. 78   Painting a base coat then outlining the scroll

Fig. 79   Adding layers of darker shades to build up a realistic appearance

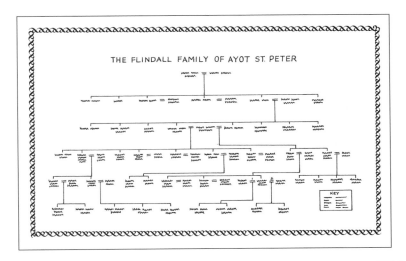

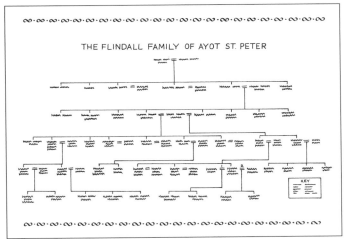

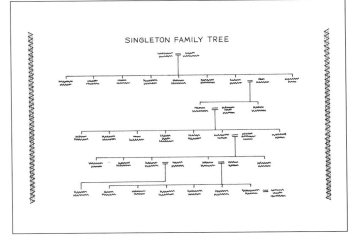

Fig. 80 Borders

benefit from borders placed on the long edges so that the chart is given more width and therefore has a less extreme shape. If you have a chart in which the text forms a square shape, you can improve it with borders to the sides making it landscape in shape, or to the top and bottom making it a portrait shape. Calligraphy pens are useful for making simple narrow borders. A few examples are shown in fig. 81. A border can greatly increase the size of a piece of work, so do not choose this method of decoration if you are very limited in size.

Fig. 81 Calligraphic borders

Some people like to put the various generations of their family into historical context by including a chronological border of historical events which ties in with the dates on the chart. This is very effective on charts which go back many years and it is interesting to see at a glance what was happening in the world at the time when particular ancestors were living. If you have a border such as this to the left or right of the chart, then it usually looks better to balance with another border on the opposite side. A good idea for the opposite border is a list of reigns of the kings and queens.

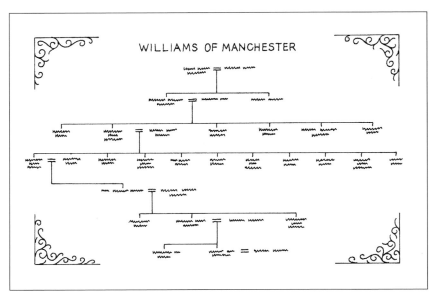

Fig. 82   Corner decoration

Corner pieces

Corner decoration is often very suitable for family trees. The majority of charts tend to widen considerably in the middle portion, leaving space in each corner as shown in fig. 82. Various forms of corner piece are shown in fig. 83. The initial design for one corner can be repeated in each corner or the design can be varied. The different corners used need not have the same sized piece of illustration. Provided you take care to make the overall effect balanced, the sizes can be made to fit the available space.

Illustrations

All sorts of illustrations can be incorporated on family trees. There is usually a wealth of suitable subjects connected with place names associated with the family. Small pictures and postcards of churches, houses, towns etc. can be used simply by tracing the part of the picture required and, if necessary,y reducing or enlarging the size of the tracing on a photocopier. Most high-street printers have photocopiers which have this facility. The tracing can then be transferred onto the chart before adding background colours and outlines. You need not be a great artist

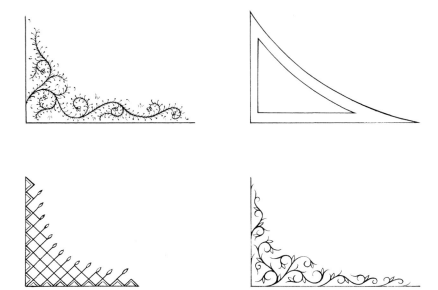

Fig. 83   Corner designs

to undertake something of this sort; it just requires a little patience and imagination to pick suitable subject matter and then careful working to reproduce the picture as accurately as possible on your chart.

Water-colour paints are preferable to gouache for illustrations of this type. A small box of a dozen or so colours should enable you to produce a pleasant picture resembling the original. The degree of

Tilly Manor

Fig. 84 Boxed illustrations, for a more formal look, especially suitable with boxed framework charts (p.64) and those containing heraldry. A boxed picture will be more prominent on the chart

detail will be dictated by your own ability and taste, but sometimes the simplest illustrations can be the most effective.

Always begin by drawing the picture on tracing paper or thin layout paper. Do not draw directly onto the chart as you will want to make corrections and this often results in an untidy mess of unclean lines. Do all this work on the draft paper; then transfer the drawing, either by tracing or with transfer paper, onto the work so that you have a clean outline to work with. The colours can then be worked into the picture and there is no need for any rubbing out on the actual chart.

Sometimes it is better to contain the illustration within a box as shown in fig.84. On other occasions it might be more appropriate to allow the illustration to sit freely on the page with no fixed boundaries, as shown in fig. 85.

Pen and ink drawings can be used instead of water-colours; their advantage is that they generally blend better with the rest of the chart. They are usually easier to produce than water-colours. If you want to use background colour washes with the line drawing it is better to trace down the outline, as explained above, and then put the colour washes onto the tracing. Wait until the washes are completely dry before making the pen and ink outlines. This should be the final step, as quite a few inks will run if the wash touches them. Rotring ink is waterproof when dry, so the outlines can be done before the washes are added. Rotring pens are very good for making line drawings as they are easy to use and the pen does not need to be constantly refilled with ink.

Pencil crayons can be used, if you are happier with this medium, and the colours

Royton Manor

Fig. 85 Unboxed illustrations, for a softer more subtle appearance, giving the effect of blending into the background. Use if the illustration is of secondary importance to the text or if the subject matter has no obvious boundary (ie. a boat on the sea, landscapes, etc.).

are usually light fast. If you intend to have the work framed, make sure to include a mount or a slip under the glass. This will keep the glass away from the crayon to which it might otherwise stick (see chapter 8).

Photographs

Researchers often collect photographs of family members and wish to incorporate them onto the chart. Rather than using old precious photographs, have copies made for use on your chart. It is difficult to introduce photographs onto this sort of work without their looking terribly out of place. Thicker photographic paper and stronger colours do not blend with the

paper of the chart. To make photographs look as if they 'belong' on the chart, give them frames in which to sit, as shown in fig. 86. There is a tendency for the photographs to appear to jump out of the page at you but with this method they do appear to be fixed in position.

Small rectangular photographs can be included in their entirety, but often with larger photographs a better effect is achieved by cutting out the relevant part. Be very careful with the cutting as uneven edges will spoil the look of the work.

Heraldry is another way of illustrating your chart. As the subject is quite involved, it has been treated separately in the following chapter.

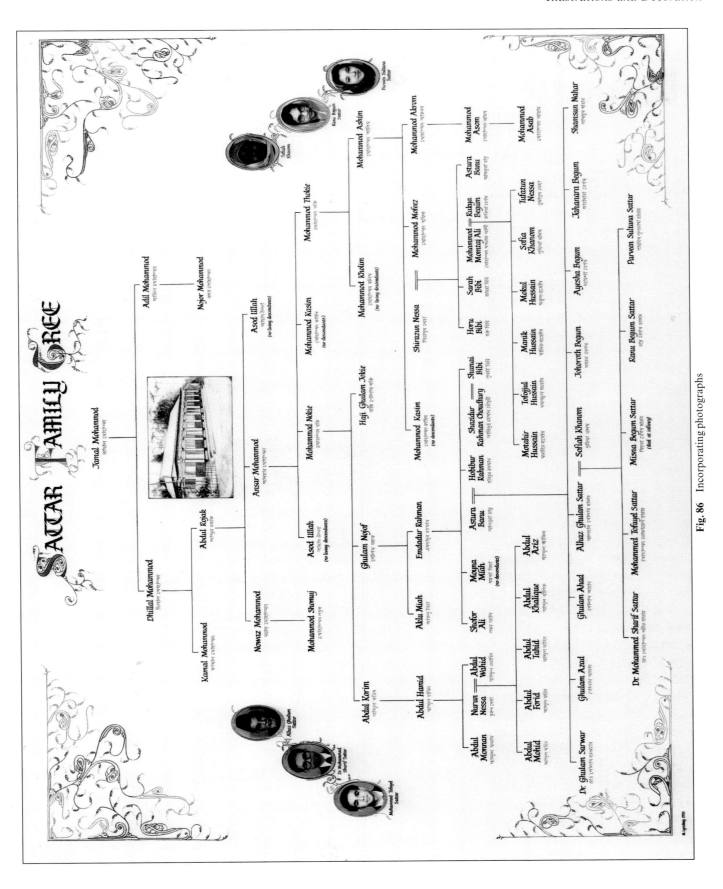

Fig. 86   Incorporating photographs

Chapter 5
Heraldry

Heraldry forms a traditional accompaniment to family history charts. If you are lucky enough to have a family coat of arms to illustrate the work, this is an obvious choice of chart decoration. Far fewer people are genuinely entitled to a coat of arms than may be imagined and the misuse of heraldry is widespread.

If your family is entitled to a coat of arms, then it is usually already a known fact as the design will appear on some of the family possessions such as china, ornaments etc. You may even be lucky enough to possess the original grant of arms. This is the vellum document granted, in the case of English subjects, by the College of Arms and signed by the Kings of Arms. The newly-granted arms appear in the top left corner of the document; along the top border are a number of smaller coats of arms. A current document issued by the College of Arms shows first, from left to right, the arms of the Earl Marshal, who is the head of the establishment, then those of the sovereign who gives authority for the grant, followed by those of the College of Arms. The text of the document takes the form of an address, to all who care to hear, by the officers of the College of Arms proclaiming that authority has been granted for the displaying by the recipient of the arms detailed therein. The document is signed at the bottom by the Kings of Arms and the large red wax seals of the officers are added.

Once a coat of arms has been granted it can be passed from father to son. Daughters can also make use of the family arms, and nowadays women in general do not have arms granted to them. (Sarah Ferguson and Margaret Thatcher are recent notable examples.) It is possible to search for a coat of arms for your own family in the hope that one may exist to which you happen to be entitled. More often you will discover nothing more than the arms of another family with the same surname. You might take the view that any family bearing your surname was at some stage, in the mists of time, connected with your own and must be a branch of your family. This is unlikely and is not acceptable to the principals of heraldry. Coats of arms are the personal property of the original grantee and his direct descendants. If a person poaches another family's coat of arms and makes free use of it, it is no better than inventing a coat of arms and using it without any authority.

The correct procedure, if you wish to acquire a coat of arms, is to approach the College of Arms in London or Lyon Court, Edinburgh for new arms to be granted. In spite of the cost, a surprisingly large number of people apply every year new to have arms granted. It is not difficult to understand why, after having the arms designed, reproduced by an artist, engrossed by a scribe, signed by the Kings of Arms, the grantee would be annoyed to see his or her personal design usurped by someone else with the same surname.

Having discussed entitlement to coats of arms, it remains to be said that good use can still be made of heraldry even if you do not have a personal entitlement. For a start, a great deal of heraldry exists for schools and colleges, civic authorities, corporate bodies etc. and you should be able to find a coat of arms in which you can claim an interest and use this association to enliven your chart. There is no reason why you should not use, say, the arms of the county or town in which you were born or of a school at which you were educated. Write the relevant details underneath the shield and you have an interesting and informative piece of decoration on the chart.

If you feel compelled to include a coat of arms which belongs to a family of the same surname but to which you have no entitlement, then include underneath the illustration a short explanation of the person to whom the arms belong, when they were granted etc. Some people include several variants of the relevant surname to show how different families of the same name have adopted and adapted different coats of arms over the years.

The achievement

A full coat of arms is known as an achievement and is divided into various parts. The arms are described in heraldic language called blazon. The names of each section are described below. Fig. 87 shows the component parts of an achievement of arms.

Shield – The shield is the main and most important part of the achievement. It can be shown alone without any of the accompanying material. The shield identifies the bearer and the heralds at the College of Arms take care that no two coats of arms are the same. For this reason, though many of the oldest coats of arms are very simple in design, these days, when it is much more difficult to come up with an original design, the designs tend to become complex. Many different shapes have been used for shields over the centuries, and there is no rule governing the shape you use. A standard shield shape with good proportions is shown in fig. 88a. The shield is simply constructed using a ruler and compasses. Draw a straight line the length you require for the top edge of the shield then rule lines down at right angles from each end one third of the length of the top line. Open the compasses to the length of the top line but place the compass point at the end of one of the short lines and mark off an arc downwards from the end of the short line on the opposite side. Repeat with an arc from the other short line, making sure that the arcs cross to form the base point of the shield. When you are ready to do the artwork, ruling pens and compasses can be used to give a strong accurate outline. If you have a shield with a lot of detail, particularly in the base area, it may be easier to use a squarer-shaped shield, as shown in fig. 88b or 88c, which will prevent the bottom part from being crammed into a curving base section. If you prefer to use a more elaborate shaped shield, such as that shown in fig. 88d, there is no reason why not, but avoid shapes with too many embellishments unless you are confident of drawing the outline accurately.

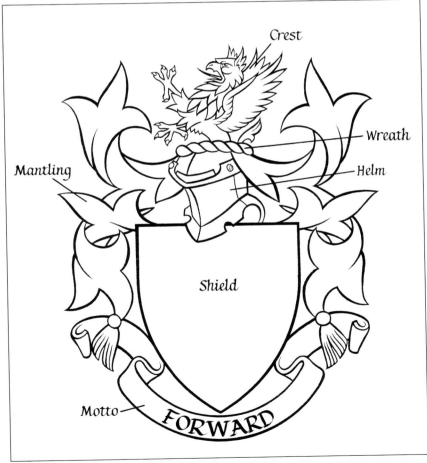

Fig. 87 Parts of a coat of arms

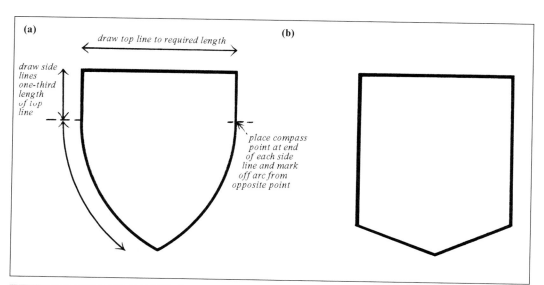

Fig. 88 (a) Standard shield shape; (b) Shield shape for crowded designs; (c) Squarer shaped shield for complicated design; (d) Unusually shaped shield

(a)

draw top line to required length

(b)

draw side lines one-third length of top line

place compass point at end of each side line and mark off arc from opposite point

VERITATEM · AMO

THE ARMORIAL BEARINGS OF
CHARLES EDWARD NIX ESQUIRE

VAUDIN ⚜ VODIN ⚜ VALDEN
Isle of Jersey

Helm – the helmet or helm most commonly used is the esquire's helm shown in fig. 89a. It is shown facing to the left, either completely in profile or angled slightly as in the example. There are various other forms of helm used to denote rank. A knight or baronet for instance uses a forward facing helm with an open visor, fig. 89b. Peers have other different designs depending on their rank. On top of the helm sits the crest wreath or torse which is usually composed of two,

Fig. 89 Helms

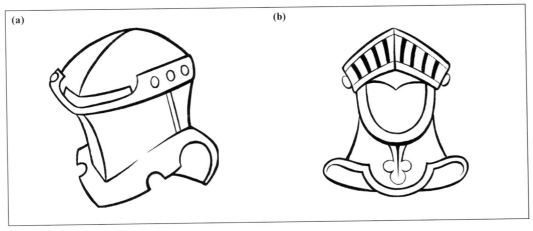

(a)   (b)

sometimes three, interwoven bands in different colours. The colours are usually the principal two mentioned in the blazon. If the colours of the wreath, differ from the principal colours, they will be separately described.

Crest – the crest is the part of the achievement which sits upon the crest wreath on the helm. Sometimes you will find that a crown or a cap will be used instead of a wreath, but the wreath is most frequently met with. The crest may be derived from the items composing the shield or it can be a totally unrelated object. Crests are usually drawn to reflect the direction of the helm, so that a crest on an esquire's helm will face to the left as does the helm. This can lead to a few problems with some objects which naturally ought to be shown facing forwards. A little artistic licence can therefore be employed to turn the helm slightly forward and the crest slightly to the left. The crest, like the shield, is often used alone; this has unfortunately led to the description 'family crest' being used by many of the uninformed when in fact they mean the whole achievement. The crest is only the object placed above the helmet on the crest wreath. It is not necessary to show the helm with the crest, and crests on their own are frequently used on seal rings, where the whole achievement would have made a very complex design for a small area. The crest is usually drawn at about half the height of the shield.

Mantling – this consists of a mass of curling material, usually arranged symmetrically, to left and right of the helm and shield, and issuing from the crest wreath. The origin was as a covering to protect the wearer of a helmet from the heat of the sun. The original cloth draped around the head has now evolved into a stylised arrangement of twists and turns. The colours, as with the wreath, are taken from the principal colours of the blazon. Again, it is possible to have different coloured mantling or even 'party' coloured mantling in which each strip is divided into two or more colours. The outer surface of the mantling is its principal colour. The reverse side or lining is the secondary colour and this colour is described as doubled. A blue mantling with a gold lining would therefore be described as azure doubled or (see heraldic colours).

Motto – a motto is not often included in the blazon as it is a fairly flexible part of the achievement. It is not necessary to keep to a fixed motto although in practice most armigerous families (those who are entitled to bear arms) keep a motto through generations and it is as much a fixed and recognised part of the arms as the shield itself. Sometimes two mottoes are included, one below and one above the rest of the achievement. In Scotland the practice of placing the motto above the shield and crest is favoured.

Fig. 90 Supporters

Fig. 91 Badge

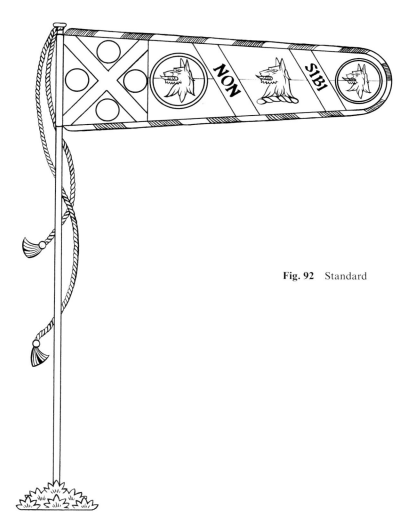

Fig. 92 Standard

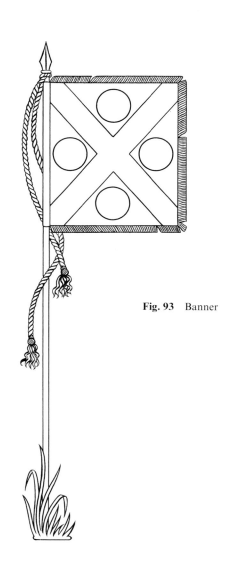

Fig. 93 Banner

Some other heraldic devices which you are likely to come across are listed below:

Supporters – these are large figures, creatures or objects to left and right of the shield, actually supporting it with their weight (fig. 90). Supporters are often given a platform on which to stand and this is termed a compartment.

Badge – heraldic badges are small personal emblems often incorporating elements of the arms (fig. 91). A patent may be separately issued for the granting of the right to display a heraldic badge, or it may be included on the original grant of arms.

Standard – this is a type of flag in a long narrow shape with a rounded end as shown in fig. 92. The standard is composed of various parts of the achievement; the full arms are usually shown next to the pole, and the background of the remaining part is often divided into the colours. If a motto is to be included, this is placed on diagonal bands across the standard; the crest is then placed in the three gaps between these bands. If the owner of the arms also has a badge, this is alternated with the crest in the gaps. The whole standard is fringed with the colours of the mantling and set on a pole, usually tasselled and set in a mound.

Banner – this is a rectangular representation of the arms on a long pole (fig. 93). Again the pole usually has a long cord with tassels at the ends flying from the top and is set on a small compartment or grassy mound.

Decorations and items denoting official status can sometimes be included in an achievement of arms. The Sovereign's arms, for example, contain the Order of the Garter encircling the shield. Most chains of office are shown in this manner, encircling the whole shield. The arms of the Earl Marshal show two batons of his office crossed behind the shield. Most decorations are shown with the ribbon encircling the shield so that the actual award hangs below the motto scroll.

Different countries employ very different sets of rules from those which govern British heraldry, so if you come across a coat of arms with unusual components which do not conform to the descriptions above then you will have to consult text books on foreign heraldry to determine what is involved in their display.

Designing Arms

If you wish to establish your own coat of arms, there are rules to be observed about the component parts. Firstly the colours or substances used to make up the design are divided into three groups – colours, metals and furs. The main heraldic colours, each having its own heraldic description, are as follows; red –gules, blue – azure, black – sable, green –vert, purple – purpure, brown – marron, orange – tenné. There are a few less frequently used colours such as blood red – sanguine, and sky blue – bleu celeste.

The metals are simply gold – or, and silver – argent. If metallic colours are not available then gold is shown as yellow and silver is shown as white, so it is up to the individual to choose which is preferred for a painting.

The furs are ermine which is stoat fur and vair which is squirrel fur. Both furs are shown in formalised patterns and several variations have been adopted and given separate names. Fig. 94a shows the usual pattern for vair; the segments are alternately white and grey. Counter-vair (fig. 94b) uses an alternative arrangement of the two colours. Straightforward ermine (fig. 94c) is black markings (representing the tip of the stoat's tail) on a white background. Ermines (fig. 94d) reverses the colours. There are special names for black and gold variations too.

When combining elements of a coat of arms a colour is not usually placed on a colour, nor a metal on a metal, nor a fur on another fur. It is acceptable to place two colours, metals or furs side by side. Objects may be shown on a coat of arms in any of the heraldic colours or they can appear in their natural colour, in which case they are termed proper. An object which is proper may appear on top of any metal, colour or fur.

Shields are usually divided into various colours by recognised dividing lines; those most frequently met with are illustrated in fig. 95. The background, which is referred to as the 'field', can have various shapes placed on it which are named in keeping with the dividing lines (fig. 96). These shapes are known in heraldry as 'ordinaries', and you will find pages of the many different variations listed in heraldic textbooks. A field can be divided by a series of the same type of lines, and these are named in a similar manner to the partition lines (fig. 97). The field of a shield is always mentioned first in the blazon before the rest of the description.

The dividing lines need not be straight; there are recognised descriptions for many different patterns of partition line, some of which are shown in fig. 98.

Charges – any item placed upon a shield is called a 'charge' and you will see in written descriptions the phrase 'charged with a ————'. For example, the blazon 'Argent a chevron gules charged with a feather or' would be 'A gold feather on a red chevron which is on a silver background'. A limitless array of charges has been used over the years. Some are always shown in a stylised heraldic form such as the seax, which is a particular shape of sword, the martlet which is a swallow always shown without feet, or the maunch which is the sleeve of a lady's gown (fig. 99). Others are simple, easily recognisable shapes with special heraldic names, such as the roundel (a circle), the billet (a rectangle) and the pierced mullet (a star with a hole in the centre), fig. 100. These days all sorts of charges are used, but simpler shapes always make more striking designs. Remember, however, that one of the problems with a new design is

(a) **Vair**   (b) **Counter-vair**

(c) **Ermine**   (d) **Ermines**

Fig. 94 Heraldic furs

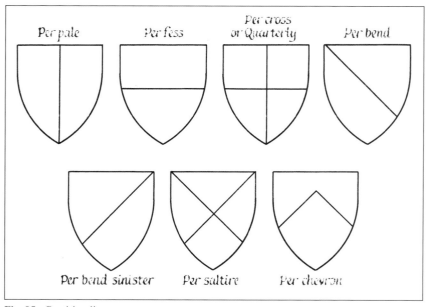

Per pale   Per fess   Per cross or Quarterly   Per bend

Per bend sinister   Per saltire   Per chevron

Fig. 95 Partition lines

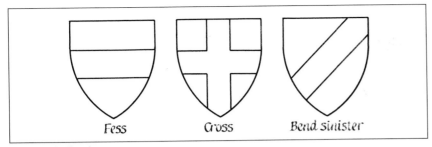

Fig. 96 Ordinaries

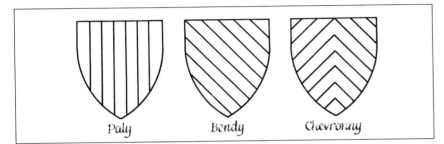

Fig. 97 Further divisions of the field

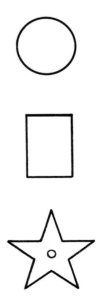

Fig. 99 Stylised heraldic charges

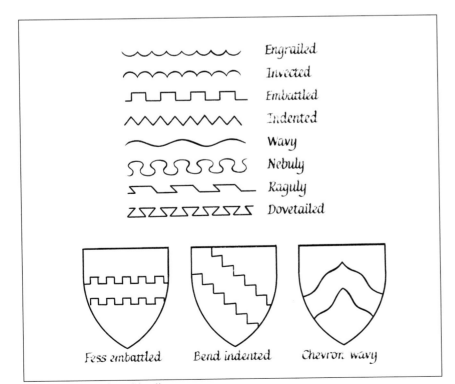

Fig. 98 Patterned partition lines

Fig. 100 Simple heraldic charges

that it will only be allowed by the Kings of Arms if it is sufficiently different from any existing design. The necessity for new designs has therefore led in recent times to a tendency towards complicated designs with very unusual charges; but, provided the design is approved by the Kings of Arms, you are free to choose.

Armigerous females

An unmarried daughter may show her father's coat of arms upon a lozenge. A lozenge is a diamond-shaped device which takes the place of a shield, as illustrated in fig. 101. The lozenge is surmounted by a ribbon called a true love knot. The arms of a married woman, if she is an heraldic heiress (having no brothers), may be *impaled* with the husband as shown in fig. 102a. Sometimes the two coats of arms are joined together (as in the example), so

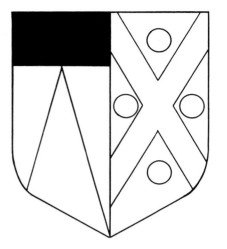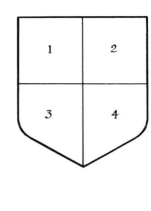

Fig. 102 (a) Impaled arms; (b) Numbering of sections of quartered arms

that each side is a narrower version of the separate shields. Alternatively, the two shields can be joined together as if each had been cut in half and put side by side. This latter method lends itself to some coats of arms rather than others, as on occasions it removes some of the charges and therefore makes the shield difficult to identify. Another method of combining the arms of husband and wife is by quartering. The shield is divided into four and the arms of the husband are placed in the first and fourth quarters (fig. 102b) and the arms of the wife in the second and third quarters. Each quarter represents a house and subsequent marriages with heriresses may lead to some complex coats of arms with many quarterings amongst great families. This makes for a very interesting genealogical history but detracts from the original purpose of the coat of arms as a means of easily distinguishing a particular family. There are several other ways in which the arms of a husband and wife can be shown, and it is best to seek advice from the heralds at the College of Arms if you intend to use the arms in formal display.

Fig. 101 Lozenge for an unmarried daughter

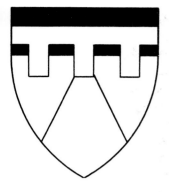

Fig. 103 Label for the eldest son

Fig. 104 Cadency marks (*from top*): label, crescent, mullet, martlet, annulet.

Cadency Marks

The sons of an armigerous person are entitled to use the father's coat of arms with a series of distinguishing marks called cadency marks. A cadency mark is placed upon the shield, usually in the top centre, and its shape denotes to which child the arms refer. The eldest son bears a label, which is a horizontal band with three or sometimes five vertical strips hanging from it. Fig. 103 shows an eldest son's label upon a shield. Fig. 104 shows the first five cadency marks; after them come a fleur-de-lis for a sixth son, a rose for a seventh son, a cross moline for an eighth son and a double quatrefoil for a ninth son.

Incorporating heraldry into a family tree

To include a coat of arms on a family tree chart you need to decide how large to make the design and how much detail you want. For example, you can use the whole achievement or only the shield or crest. There is often a space in the top left-hand corner of most charts which can be adapted to make room for a coat of arms (fig. 105). Another good position is in the top centre of the chart, with the title arranged to left and right (fig. 106). If you wish to include a number of coats of arms, they can be placed at regular intervals throughout the text, as shown in fig. 107.

Method of Painting

When you have decided on the size of the coat of arms, it must be drawn on layout paper, as with any illustration, so that it can be transferred to the chart with minimal marking of the paper surface. If you are using a helmet and crest as well as the shield, it is usual to make these two items together about the same height as the height of the shield. Coats of arms with top-heavy crests look very silly as do those with tiny crests upon a minuscule helm. It is a good idea to sketch the twists and turns of the mantling on one side of the

shield, then turn over the tracing paper and trace the same pattern on the other side. If the curves are well formed, the mirror image will make the complete mantling look very good. You will have to adjust the parts that meet with the helm so that the mantling looks as if it all stems from underneath the wreath. Use compasses to draw the main part of the motto scroll, if required; then draw one end-curl and use tracing paper to repeat the same curl at the other end. Experiment with the lettering to make sure that you choose a lettering size that will enable all the words to fit comfortably. Transfer the completed drawing to the chart using transfer or tracing paper. It is now ready to paint.

Gouache colours are best for this sort of painting, where bold, even colours are required. Try to keep to obvious colours, rather than pale pastel shades, or those which are not immediately obvious, such as turquoise, which can be mistaken for blue or green. Mix a colour to the consistency of thin cream—not thin enough to be transparent, but not so thick as to form ridges when it dries. The desired effect is an even covering with no blotchy patches. Once the transferred outline of the drawing is in place on the chart, paint each of the base colours until all of the design has its first covering of paint. If you prefer to use metallic gold and silver rather than white or yellow these are available in tubes of gouache. Metallic gold is always very effective but I tend not to use silver as it gives a stark or overdone appearance to the whole painting when used on large areas.

The next step is to outline the various parts. Avoid using black as this gives the picture a very hard appearance. A deep brown colour, obtained by mixing equal quantities of black and bright red, makes a very good outlining colour. Other colours might be suggested by the dominant colours of the arms. For example, a shield principally in green and

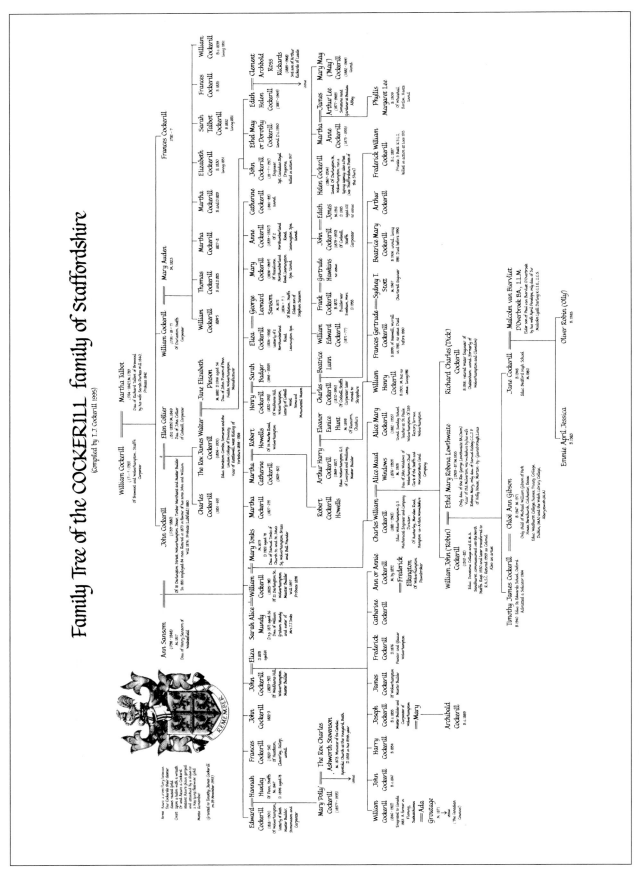

Fig. 105   Making room for a coat of arms in a top corner

gold might best be outlined in dark green. If possible use a ruling pen and compasses for the shield and the central part of the motto scroll. The crisp lines given by these instruments really improve the painting. Take care when you rule over the top of other painted areas, as the paint flows out more quickly than when the pen touches unpainted paper. Experiment first by painting a small square on a practice-sheet. Fill the ruling pen and rule along one of the outside lines. The paint should come out in a nice sharp line. Do not overfill the ends of the ruling pen or you will start with a large blob of paint. If you fill too little paint it will be difficult to make it come out. Try all four sides of the square to perfect the technique. When the paint has dried, fill the pen again and this time draw a line right across the square. This time you should find that the paint runs out much more quickly onto the completely painted area and the line is thicker and less sharp. For this reason it is better to narrow the gap between the points of the pen when ruling right over painted areas. Make sure you clean the ruling pen every time you have finished a group of lines, and have to wait before completing the rest, as the paint will dry very quickly in the pen and clog it. Keep a scrap of paper at the side of the work and draw a short line each time you have filled the pen, to make sure that the paint is flowing smoothly before you place it on the work. After outlining, further detail can be added where required and a three dimensional effect can be built up with successive layers of blended shades of the base colour as described on page 42.

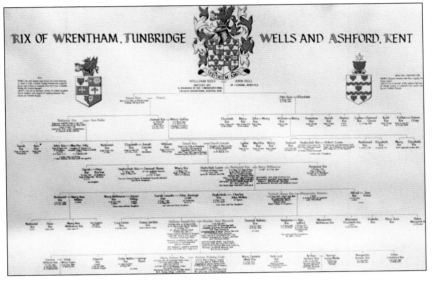

Fig. 106 *(above)* Positioning a coat of arms at the top centre of a chart

Fig. 107 *(right)* Dispersing shields throughout the text

Hatching

When it is not possible to use colour, a system of lines and dots has been devised to represent the different heraldic colours. This system is known as hatching and the colours are illustrated in fig. 108. You will see these colours appear in seals, on bookplates and on printed black and white illustrations of arms.

Using bright colours and strong shapes, heraldry is a very effective accompaniment to the family tree.

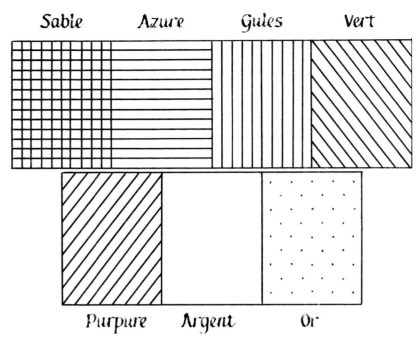

Fig. 108   Hatching

Fig. 109   Broadsheet of coats of arms related to one family

Chapter 6
Alternative Layouts

There are other ways of laying out a family tree apart from using the drop-line format or birth brief style described in chapter 2.

Circles and semi-circles

Circular and semi-circular formats can be used for family trees, as shown in fig. 110. The main subject (or subjects) of the whole chart is placed in the centre of the circle. The next ring is divided into two and each of the parents occupy one of the two halves. The next ring is divided into four and used for the grandparents and so on, going out to as many rings as required. Although this method is quite attractive,

easy to follow and space saving, there are several disadvantages. The main one is that it is only practical for birth-brief type charts where just the direct ancestors of the main person need to be shown. A second disadvantage is that there is little space for including biographical detail and the amount available decreases the further from the centre you go. It is therefore a good idea to increase the depth of each ring so that there is more room available for dates of birth etc (fig. 111a). By the time you have reached a 6th or 7th ring from the centre it is necessary to deepen the rings a great deal and to write the text on straight lines along each segment (fig. 111b). The third disadvantage of the circular method is that, if all the lettering faces inwards, many names appear upside down. To avoid this the top half of the circle can be written with the names arching upwards and the bottom half with the names arching downwards. With the outer rings, where the text is written in straight lines, the change, from writing the text inwards to writing it outwards, occurs at the top and bottom of the chart as shown in fig. 111b. Semi-circular charts use exactly the same method, but over the diameter of a half circle as in fig. 112.

It is possible to make a circular chart to include families of brothers and sisters of the main descendants, but it is necessary to form the tree in the opposite direction to the above method. The oldest known ancestors are placed in the centre of the

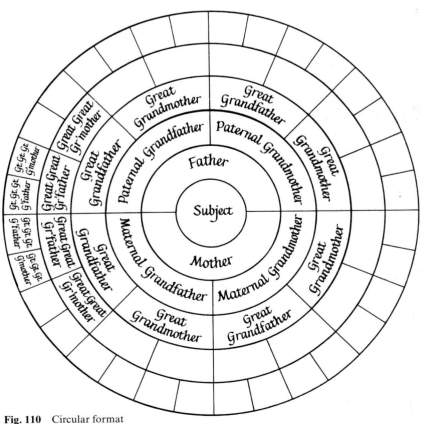

Fig. 110   Circular format

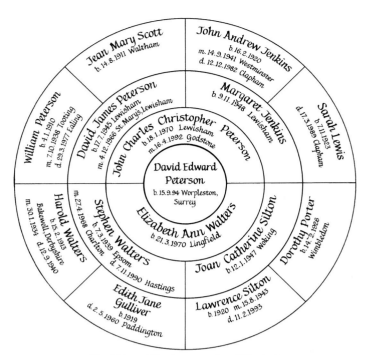

Fig. 111a   Allowing room for all the text

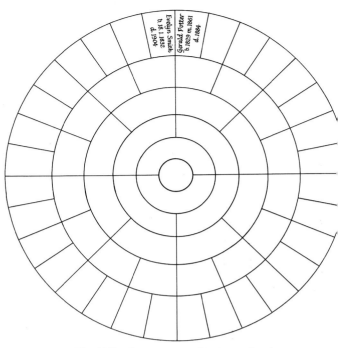

Fig. 111b   Arrangement of text on outer rings

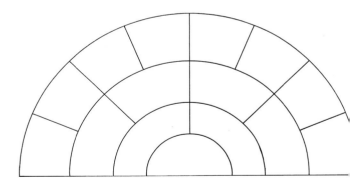

Fig. 112   Semicircular format

circle with their descendants radiating outwards in circles. This method works well in that, as you spread out further, you have more room each time for the growing number of descendants which occur in most charts. The main drawback of this method is the need to adjust the direction in which each name faces to enable the text to be easily read without constantly turning the chart (fig. 113). Try to keep the names in the top half curving upwards and those in the bottom half curving downwards. In the sample it was possible to arrange most of the family groups so that all the names appeared in the same direction. The only exception was for the three children of Daniel and Esther. All three children could have been written facing outwards, but then Anthony's entry would have been very difficult to read and also out of keeping with the rest of the top of the chart. Such decisions are a matter of personal preference.

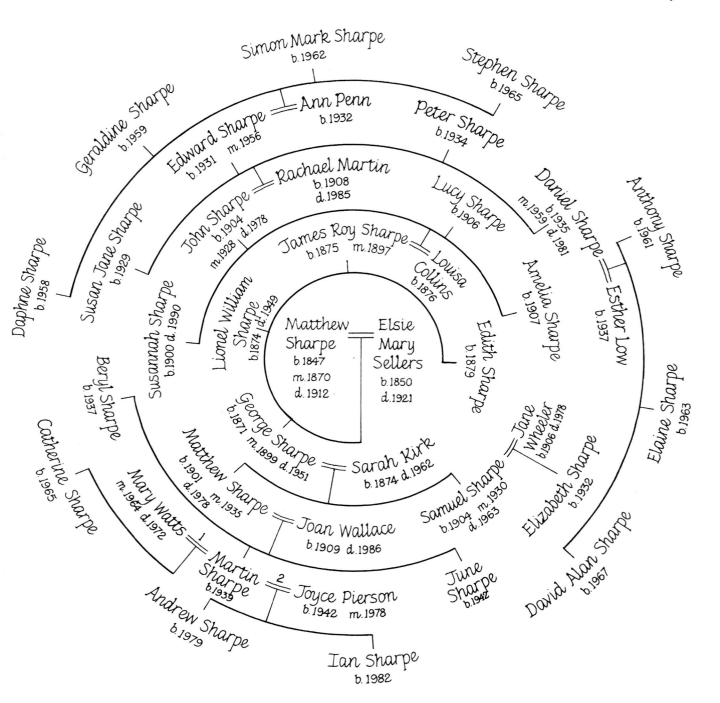

Fig. 113 Circular chart including complete families

Boxed frameworks

A very neat appearance can be achieved by enclosing the information for different members of a family within individual boxes or circles linked together by a framework of lines (fig. 114). This is a variation of the drop-line pedigree. It has a drawback in that the amount of space required is far greater than for ordinary drop-line charts, but it can give a very clear, easy to follow chart.

Some people like to use boxes for the males of the family and circles for the females (fig. 115). You will need a ruling pen and compasses to draw all the boxes and circles accurately. If you want to keep

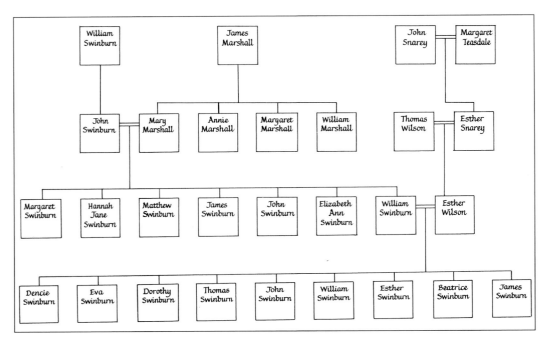

Fig. 114 Boxed framework chart

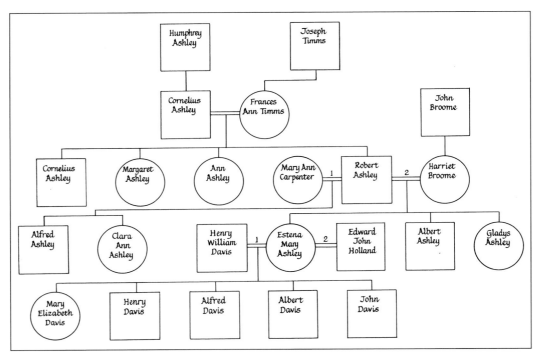

Fig. 115 Box and circle framework

the proportions of all the boxes or circles the same, remember to check that the largest amount of information for any person will fit the size of box you choose. The longest entry must be made to fit first, so that you establish a size for all the others. It pays to write in rough first all the information for each person to ensure that all the lettering will be well spaced in each box.

Direct-Line Descent

If you decide to chart only a direct line of descent through one branch of the family, you will have a long narrow chart (fig. 116a). To counteract this, write the names on single lines only. Use the minimum number of lines possible for the biographical details, making what information there is occupy the whole width of the name to which it belongs, or longer if necessary. Figs. 116(b) and (c) show how the text of an entry can be adapted to suit the layout. Example (b) is much better for the direct line of descent whereas (c) would suit a wider chart. Fig. 117 shows how blocks of narrative text and illustrations have been placed alongside a narrow direct-line descent to give a balanced effect.

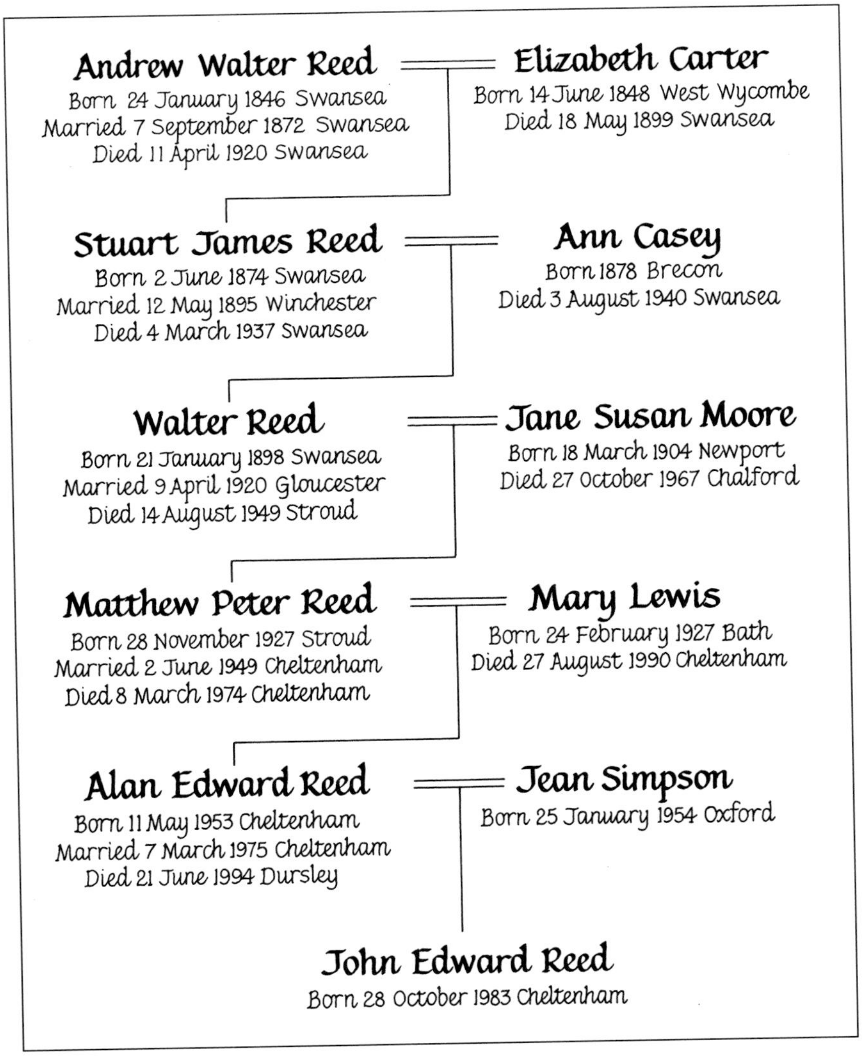

Andrew Walter Reed ══ **Elizabeth Carter**
Born 24 January 1846 Swansea / Born 14 June 1848 West Wycombe
Married 7 September 1872 Swansea / Died 18 May 1899 Swansea
Died 11 April 1920 Swansea

Stuart James Reed ══ **Ann Casey**
Born 2 June 1874 Swansea / Born 1878 Brecon
Married 12 May 1895 Winchester / Died 3 August 1940 Swansea
Died 4 March 1937 Swansea

Walter Reed ══ **Jane Susan Moore**
Born 21 January 1898 Swansea / Born 18 March 1904 Newport
Married 9 April 1920 Gloucester / Died 27 October 1967 Chalford
Died 14 August 1949 Stroud

Matthew Peter Reed ══ **Mary Lewis**
Born 28 November 1927 Stroud / Born 24 February 1927 Bath
Married 2 June 1949 Cheltenham / Died 27 August 1990 Cheltenham
Died 8 March 1974 Cheltenham

Alan Edward Reed ══ **Jean Simpson**
Born 11 May 1953 Cheltenham / Born 25 January 1954 Oxford
Married 7 March 1975 Cheltenham
Died 21 June 1994 Dursley

John Edward Reed
Born 28 October 1983 Cheltenham

Fig. 116a Direct line of descent

(a)

Andrew Walter Reed
Born 24 January 1846 Swansea
Married 7 September 1872 Swansea
Died 11 April 1920 Swansea

(b)

Andrew Walter
Reed
Born 24 January 1846
Swansea
Married 7 September 1872
Swansea
Died 11 April 1920
Swansea

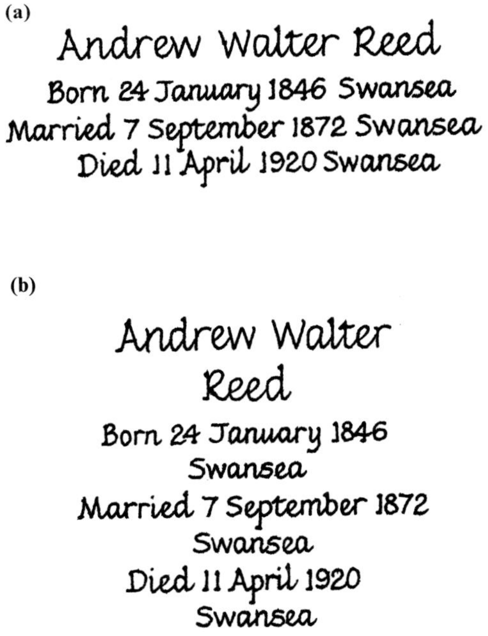

Fig. 116b & c Adapting text to suit layout

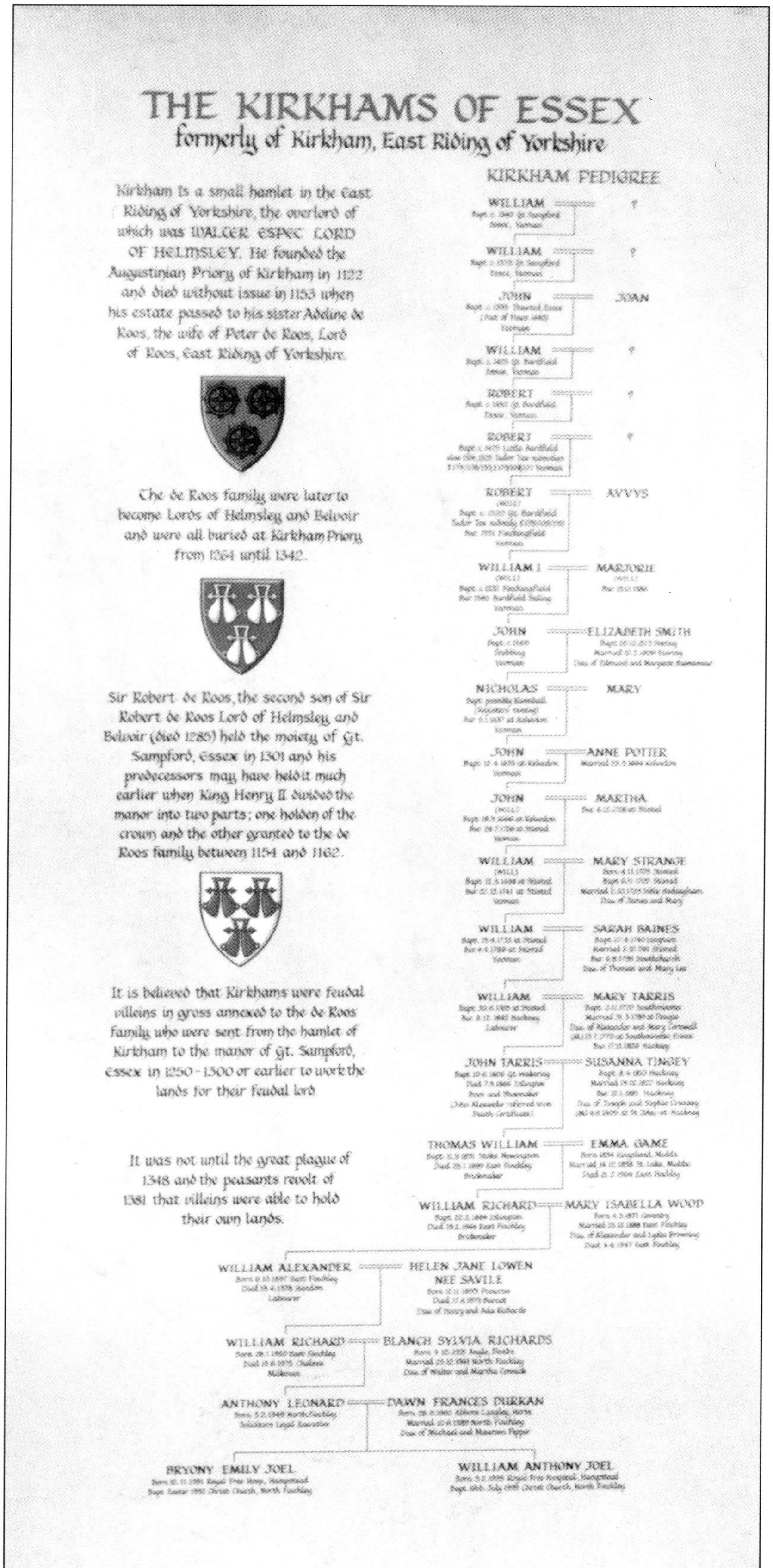

THE KIRKHAMS OF ESSEX
formerly of Kirkham, East Riding of Yorkshire

Kirkham is a small hamlet in the East Riding of Yorkshire, the overlord of which was WALTER ESPEC LORD OF HELMSLEY. He founded the Augustinian Priory of Kirkham in 1122 and died without issue in 1153 when his estate passed to his sister Adeline de Roos, the wife of Peter de Roos, Lord of Roos, East Riding of Yorkshire.

The de Roos family were later to become Lords of Helmsley and Belvoir and were all buried at Kirkham Priory from 1264 until 1342.

Sir Robert de Roos, the second son of Sir Robert de Roos Lord of Helmsley and Belvoir (died 1285) held the moiety of Gt. Sampford, Essex in 1301 and his predecessors may have held it much earlier when King Henry II divided the manor into two parts; one holden of the crown and the other granted to the de Roos family between 1154 and 1162.

It is believed that Kirkhams were feudal villeins in gross annexed to the de Roos family who were sent from the hamlet of Kirkham to the manor of Gt. Sampford, Essex in 1250-1300 or earlier to work the lands for their feudal lord.

It was not until the great plague of 1348 and the peasants revolt of 1381 that villeins were able to hold their own lands.

KIRKHAM PEDIGREE

WILLIAM — ?

WILLIAM — ?

JOHN — JOAN

WILLIAM — ?

ROBERT — ?

ROBERT — ?

ROBERT — AVVYS

WILLIAM I — MARJORIE

JOHN — ELIZABETH SMITH

NICHOLAS — MARY

JOHN — ANNE POTTER

JOHN — MARTHA

WILLIAM — MARY STRANGE

WILLIAM — SARAH BAINES

WILLIAM — MARY TARRIS

JOHN TARRIS — SUSANNA TINGEY

THOMAS WILLIAM — EMMA GAME

WILLIAM RICHARD — MARY ISABELLA WOOD

WILLIAM ALEXANDER — HELEN JANE LOWEN NEE SAVILE

WILLIAM RICHARD — BLANCH SYLVIA RICHARDS

ANTHONY LEONARD — DAWN FRANCES DURKAN

BRYONY EMILY JOEL   WILLIAM ANTHONY JOEL

Fig. 117 Illustrating narrow direct line descent

Fig. 118 Left to right layout

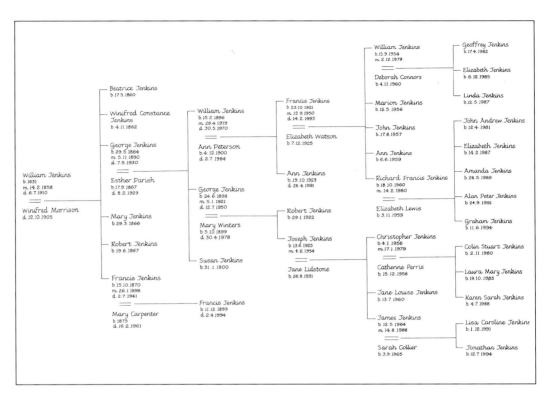

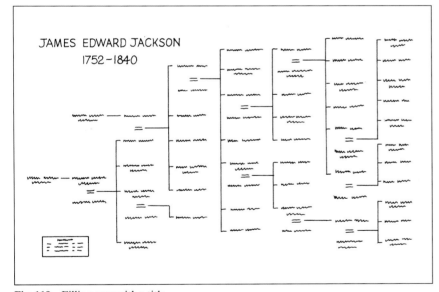

Fig. 119 Filling gaps with a title and key

Left to right layout

This is the style of chart used for the birth brief but it can easily be adapted to take as many additional relatives as required. It has a great advantage over all other layout methods in that large generations are accommodated more economically because each member of a family of brothers and sisters is placed underneath the previous one rather than side by side (fig.118). The price to be paid is a chart which looks less balanced than a drop-line chart as the discrepancy in width, from one generation to the next across the page, is more pronounced from left to right than from top to bottom. This imbalance can be re-dressed by filling the gaps with the title, a key, illustrations etc. In fig. 119 the title fills the top-left gap and a small key the bottom-left gap.

The draft work on a left to right layout is reduced as the names are all placed in line with each other to the left of each column of text. It is not necessary to find out where each name starts and finishes, as you must when you centralise the information. The only part of the text to be measured is the longest name. This name will determine the width of each column of text. If you want to include a lot of biographical information with certain names, leave a suitable amount of space between names. If necessary, write the whole entry in rough first to make sure that it will fit the allotted space.

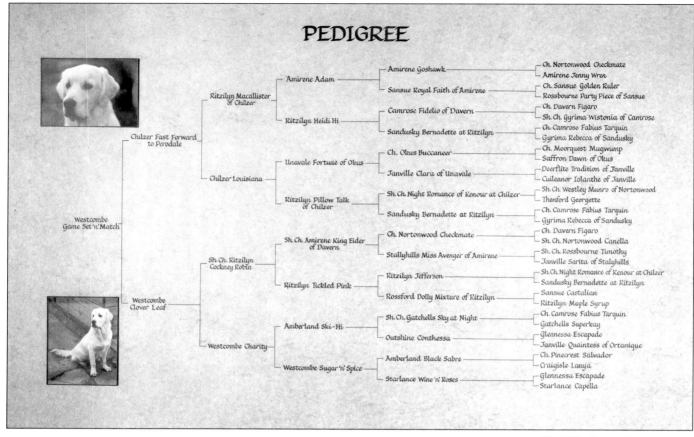

PEDIGREE

Chilzer Fast Forward to Perodale
- Ritzilyn Macallister of Chilzer
  - Amirene Adam
    - Amirene Goshawk
      - Ch. Nortonwood Checkmate
      - Amirene Jenny Wren
    - Sansue Royal Faith of Amirene
      - Ch. Sansue Golden Ruler
      - Rossbourne Party Piece of Sansue
  - Ritzilyn Heidi Hi
    - Camrose Fidelio of Davern
      - Ch. Davern Figaro
      - Sh. Ch. Gyrima Wistonia of Camrose
    - Sandusky Bernadette at Ritzilyn
      - Ch. Camrose Fabius Tarquin
      - Gyrima Rebecca of Sandusky
- Chilzer Louisiana
  - Unavale Fortune of Okus
    - Ch. Okus Buccaneer
      - Ch. Moorquest Mugwump
      - Saffron Dawn of Okus
    - Janville Clara of Unavale
      - Deerflite Tradition of Janville
      - Cuileanor Iolanthe of Janville
  - Ritzilyn Pillow Talk of Chilzer
    - Sh. Ch. Night Romance of Kenour at Chilzer
      - Sh. Ch. Westley Munro of Nortonwood
      - Thenford Georgette
    - Sandusky Bernadette at Ritzilyn
      - Ch. Camrose Fabius Tarquin
      - Gyrima Rebecca of Sandusky

Westcombe Game Set 'n' Match
Westcombe Clover Leaf
- Sh. Ch. Ritzilyn Cockney Robin
  - Sh. Ch. Amirene King Eider of Davern
    - Ch. Nortonwood Checkmate
      - Ch. Davern Figaro
      - Sh. Ch. Nortonwood Canella
    - Stallyhills Miss Avenger of Amirene
      - Sh. Ch. Rossbourne Timothy
      - Janville Sarita of Stalyhills
  - Ritzilyn Tickled Pink
    - Ritzilyn Jefferson
      - Sh. Ch. Night Romance of Kenour at Chilzer
      - Sandusky Bernadette at Ritzilyn
    - Rossford Dolly Mixture of Ritzilyn
      - Sansue Castalian
      - Ritzilyn Maple Syrup
- Westcombe Charity
  - Amberland Ski-Hi
    - Sh. Ch. Gatchells Sky at Night
      - Ch. Camrose Fabius Tarquin
      - Gatchells Superkay
    - Outshine Conthessa
      - Glennessa Escapade
      - Janville Quaintess of Ortanique
  - Westcombe Sugar 'n' Spice
    - Amberland Black Sabre
      - Ch. Pinecrest Salvador
      - Craigisle Lanya
    - Starlance Wine 'n' Roses
      - Glennessa Escapade
      - Starlance Capella

Fig. 120 Dog pedigree

Not only people have interesting pedigrees. Fig. 120 shows the genealogy of a pedigree dog using the left to right format. With dog pedigrees the accepted layout is to show the subject dog on the far left. The dog's sire and dam then follow in the next column and are linked together in a way that on a human chart would make them appear like progeny of the first dog rather than parents.

Tree-shaped and pictorial charts

Many people like to make the chart more than a network of neatly arranged lettering. To represent the family tree in tree shape has always had an appeal. Fig. 121 shows a complex tree-shaped chart including many coats of arms. The main subject is written on the trunk of the tree; the ancestors are written onto each of the branches as they radiate outwards or are hung on little scrolls on the

branches, as in the example. Some people also like to use the roots as well for some of the names. Little information can be included and the actual genealogical details tend to take second place to the whole picture, but that is all that is required of this sort of chart.

Narrative pedigrees

This type of pedigree is used in large genealogical works such as *Burke's Landed Gentry*. The chart tells the history of the family in a continuous dialogue usually on a page split into two columns to make the text easier to read. Abbreviations are used in abundance to save space and make the text flow more rapidly.

The example below is a simplified version of the method used in large genealogical works. These books usually plot a family history leading to the current head

Fig. 121 Tree-shaped chart

```
Generation A1
    Generation B1
    Generation B2
        Generation C1
    Generation B3
        Generation C1
        Generation C2
            Generation D1
                Generation E1
                    Generation F1
                    Generation F2
                    Generation F3
                Generation E2
                Generation E3
            Generation D2
                Generation E1
                    Generation F1
                Generation E2
            Generation D3
            Generation D4
                Generation E1
            Generation D5
                Generation E1
                Generation E2
    Generation B4
        Generation C1
            Generation D1
                Generation E1
                Generation E2
                Generation E3
            Generation D2
            Generation D3
        Generation C2
        Generation C3
            Generation D1
                Generation E1
            Generation D2
    Generation B5
```

Fig. 122   Formation of a narrative pedigree

```
First (oldest) generation
 ·  1.   Generation 2
 ·  2.   Generation 2
 ◆      1. Generation 3
 ·  3.   Generation 2
 ◆      1. Generation 3
 ◆      2. Generation 3
       *1. Generation 4
          • 1. Generation 5
              1. Generation 6
              2. Generation 6
              3. Generation 6
          • 2. Generation 5
          • 3. Generation 5
       *2. Generation 4
          • 1. Generation 5
              1. Generation 6
          • 2. Generation 5
       *3. Generation 4
       *4. Generation 4
          • 1. Generation 5
       *5. Generation 4
          • 1. Generation 5
          • 2. Generation 5
 ·  4.   Generation 2
 ◆      1. Generation 3
       *1. Generation 4
          • 1. Generation 5
          • 2. Generation 5
          • 3. Generation 5
       *2. Generation 4
       *3. Generation 4
 ◆      2. Generation 3
 ◆      3. Generation 3
       *1. Generation 4
          • 1. Generation 5
       *2. Generation 4
 ·  5.   Generation 2
```

Fig. 123   Adding bullet markers

of the family, and so the system treats the senior line differently from the other family members. The majority of family historians do not want to do this, preferring to give their own branch more prominence or to make all the branches of equal importance. The simplified method below will be more useful for those unfamiliar with the system.

No complex chart drawing is necessary, but a system of 'bullets' indicating each person in each generation is used. Fig. 122 shows how the system works in its simplest form. The member or members of the first (oldest) known generation appear to the left-hand side and each member of that generation is identified with the same marker, in this case an 'A', and then a number according to their order in the family. Spouses of generation 'A' members are included with the relevant family member. Children of any of these marriages will then be indented slightly from the first column of generation A members and these children will be identified as B1, B2 and so on. Each subsequent generation is treated in exactly the same way. Each person in the family must have his or her progeny listed through to the most recent members before the next person's descendants commence. You will end up with a list of all the family members in order of precedence.

Fig. 123 shows the next stage, with the bullet marks added. These are necessary to enable the reader to identify each generation in the middle of a long narrative. As the bullet markers indicate the generations more clearly, the width of the spread of names can be reduced. Use any set of bullet markers you wish or perhaps different colours to identify the different generations.

This looks straightforward when arranged in skeletal form, as shown, with no biographical detail, but anyone who has ever had to interpret a large family in *Burke's Landed Gentry* will understand how, even with the bullets in place, large amounts of detail cause confusion. A frequent mistake is not to refer back to the relevant generation when working out who is descended from whom. On involved pedigrees it can be very difficult to tell who is descended from whom once you reach the fourth or fifth generation, but by carefully following the system the method works very well. This layout is the least space consuming of all, but family relationships cannot be seen at a glance as on most other types of family history layout.

Fig. 124 provides the information from the chart in chapter 2, fig. 18 rearranged into a narrative pedigree. Each

---

Thomas Gurney Flindall
b.c.1799 Ayot St. Peter, Herts., d. 15.3.1845
Welwyn, Herts., Blacksmith, m. 16.4.1823 at
Ayot St. Peter, Jane Wells b. 1797 d.
28.4.1860 Welwyn, Herts. and had issue

- **1. John Flindall** b. 29.5.1825 Ayot St. Peter
- **2. female**
- **3. Thomas Flindall** b. 22.5.1831, d.1886 m. 31.7.1852 at Kensington, Charlotte Rodgers?
- **4. Rebecca Flindall** b.5.2.1837, m. 5.6.1858 at St. Mary's, Westminster, William O'Donnell who b.c.1835
- **5. Edward Flindall** b.20.7.1834, d.25.3.1886, Stone Mason, m.19.4.1857 at St. James, Norland, Julia Maria Hewison who d.c.1896, dau. of John Hewison, Plane Maker
  - ◆ 1. John Flindall
  - ◆ 2. Julia Maria Flindall b.1858 Westminster
  - ◆ 3. Edward Flindall b.1857
  - ◆ 4. Godfrey Martin Flindall b. 27.10.1868 Brompton, d.22.12.1919 Bromley, m. 23.4.1883 Ellen Elizabeth Andrews who b.c. 1871, d.26.12.1944
    - *1. Julia Emily Flindall b.1895
    - *2. Thomas Edward Jones Flindall b.15.8.1897 Poplar, d.31.5.1983 East Ham, m.1.8.1942 East Ham Alice Frances Yexley (nee Potter) who b. 12.11.1902 canning Town, d.10.1.1981 Smithfield
      - 1. Brian Derek Flindall b. 15.1.1943 East Ham, m.8.5.1965 Wendy Georgina Taylor
        - *1. Karen Anne Flindall* b.7.7.1970 Plaistow
        - *2. Justin William Flindall* b.26.9.1972 Rochford
      - 2. David Edward Flindall b.15.12.1944 East Ham, m.20.7.1963 Pamela Lewsey
        - *1. Paul David Flindall* b.5.1.1964
        - *2. John Barry Flindall* b.27.7.1966
        - *3. Simon Andrew Flindall* b.24.10.1972
    - *3. Ellen Elizabeth Flindall b.1899 Stepney, d. aged 33
    - *4. Robert William Flindall b.1901, d.4.10.1967, m.1934 West Ham, Gladys Ashley and had issue.
    - *5. Esther Flindall b.17.6.1903 Mile End, d.20.1.1977 Darlington, m.29.1.1930 Albert Edward Bishop who b.1902
    - *6. John Ernest Flindall b.21.6.1905 Mile End, d.15.3.1975 Leek, Staffs.,m.10.9.1932 Christina Margaret Stoddart who d.15.4.1988
      - 1. John Malcolm Flindall b.12.4.1933
      - 2. Jacqueline Flindall b.29.12.1934
    - *7. Annie Rose Flindall b.7.11.1907, d.15.9.1976 Stockton on Tees, m.9.2.1930 Thomas Edward Lilley
  - ◆ 5. Thomas Flindall b.3.10.1873 Chelsea, Captain in Merchant Navy, m.10.9.1932 West Ham as Thomas Harding his brothers widow Ellen Elizabeth Flindall nee Andrews
    - *1. Andrew Henry Flindall b.30.11.1909 Canning Town, d.1957 Romford, Sailor R.N., m.22.4.1934 St. Peters, Dagenham Mary Elizabeth Davis who b.24.6.1910 London, d.6.7.1982 Penzance
      - 1. Angela Iris Flindall b.1.10.1935 West Ham, m.15.2.1958 Staines, Thomas Patrick Lynskey who b.1.9.1935 Cramlington, Northumberland
      - 2. Irene Estena Flindall b.28.3.1942 Glasgow, m.14.7.1963 Kenneth Donald Crewe
      - 3. David Andrew Flindall b.24.2.1948 Dagenham, m.1stly Kathleen Reilly and had issue;
        - *1. Joanna Mary Flindall*
        - *2. Jaclyn Marie Flindall*
        - He m.2ndly Denise Howells and had issue;
        - *3. Christopher Flindall*
        - *4. Scott Flindall*
    - *2. Philip George Flindall b.10.11.1911, m.Jenny Stoddart
      - 1. Alan Flindall b.1932 West Ham
      - 2. Roy P. Flindall b.1939 East Ham
      - 3. Godfrey Flindall
      - 4. Denise Flindall
  - ◆ 6. Rosina Flindall
  - ◆ 7. Esther Flindall
  - ◆ 8. Robert Flindall b.1877 Poplar
- **6. Esther Flindall** b.1839, m.1860 Kensington

Fig. 124   Narrative pedigree

column or generation is distinguished by a separate series of bullets and numerals. Reading through the narrative from beginning to end, it is easy to forget the sequence, but by referring each time to the same type of bullet or numeral you will see from whom each person is descended. In fig. 124 the last person named, Esther Flindall, is the youngest child of the original Thomas Gurney Flindall, although she appears after many other people born long after her. All Esther's elder brothers and sisters and their issue, being senior in line to her as the youngest of the family, have been detailed in correct order of precedence before her. In major genealogical works sons are all listed before daughters as they usually take precedence, but your own chart can incorporate whichever method best suits you.

The best way to include a lot of material on other families connected through marriage to the main branch is to make a cross-reference to the new family alongside the entry for the person in the main family, i.e.

Robert William Flindall b.1901, d.4.10.1967, m. 1934 West Ham, Gladys Ashley (see Ashley family) and had issue.

You can then list a new family, in this case the Ashley family, under their name, again starting from the oldest known member and working through to the most recent. When you reach the person who married into the original family, the spouse is listed and cross-referenced to the first part of the narrative. If you are the type of researcher who has followed back every one of your ancestors to the point of exhaustion, this method of setting out the results of your research could be the best means of recording all the information in one place.

To return briefly to the more complex method used in major printed works, the line of descent from the earliest member to the current head of the family is emphasised by reserving the details of each head until those of less importance have been listed. The information for the family will begin by detailing the current holder of the title and his immediate family. The lineage of the whole family then begins with the oldest known member. His children will be listed using marker bullets, as previously described, but the child who is to become the next head of the family is named but without other details until all his brothers and sisters and their descendants have been listed. By reserving the details of the head of the family in each generation until all the junior branches have been dealt with, the current head will appear at the end of the narrative.

Layout – For a narrative pedigree you need to decide firstly how wide to make the columns of text. This will depend on the size of lettering. If the lettering is fairly small (say, under 3mm in height), narrow columns of no more than 10cm will make the text easy to read. If you use larger lettering, a good guide is to keep to an average of 10-15 words per line. Write out your whole family history using the bullet system described above. The easiest way is to use a typewriter or word processor rather than hand writing the text. The typed text will be an adequate guide to the number of words you can fit into each line. When your whole continuous narrative is ready, you can then decide how you will split it up into columns on the chart. For a landscape-shaped chart three columns will be better than two, as shown in fig. 125. For portrait-shaped charts two columns tend to look better (fig. 126), but it depends on how much text you have and how wide you have chosen to make the columns. A vertical rule can be placed between the columns or they can be separated by a blank margin. Subtitles for different family branches can be written in larger lettering which fits across the width of a single column, whereas your main title can spread across the combined column widths.

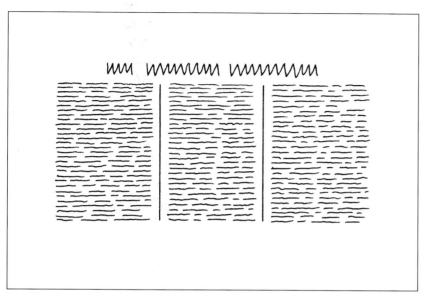

Fig. 125 Arranging text columns for a landscape format

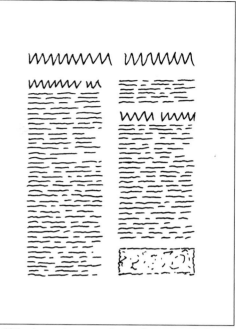

Fig. 126 Arranging text columns for a portrait format

Experiment by arranging the text on a large sheet of layout paper and, when you have arrived at a balanced arrangement, you can mark margins for the whole chart. You can be generous with margins around closely packed blocks of text, so allow a wide margin of equal depth at both sides and at the top. Make the bottom margin slightly larger for good balance. You now have the page size for the work itself, assuming that you wish to make the text the same size as the typed copy. If not, you must make an additional simple rough draft, and write out a few lines of the text in the size you wish to use so that you can see how wide your columns of text will be. When you have done this, you can calculate the length of the whole text based on the number of lines of typed text you have used. Add the margins to the newly calculated text area and you are ready to begin the final version.

When you write out the text onto the actual chart, try to keep to the number of words per line used on the typed copy. You may need to alter the text slightly to avoid spaces at ends of lines or cramped words. If, when you reach the end of the columns,

there is some space left, a small block of filler pattern will even up the columns. If the final column is too long, your filler pattern will have to be used at the bottom of the previous column(s).

One great advantage of the narrative style of family history is that a great deal of biographical detail for any member of the family can be included without occupying too much space and making the rest of the chart unbalanced.

If the bullet marker method is too confusing, you might prefer the commentary approach to the family history. With this method you write the history as if you were telling a story, for example:

'In or about 1799 Thomas Gurney Flindall was born in the village of Ayot St Peter in Hertfordshire. He was a blacksmith by trade. On 16 April 1823 he married Jane Wells. Jane was born in 1797 but her place of birth is unknown. The marriage took place at Ayot St Peter. Thomas died on 28 April 1860 at Welwyn in Hertfordshire. He left behind a family of six children the eldest of whom was

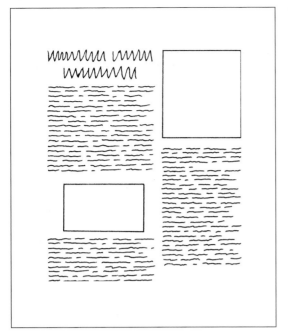

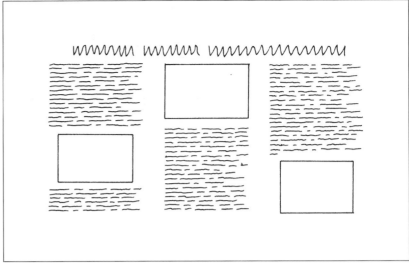

Fig. 127   Arranging blocks of text and pictures

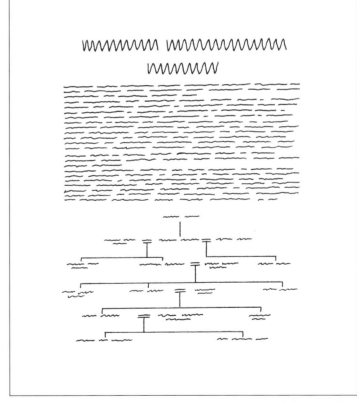

Fig. 128   Combining narrative-and drop-line pedigrees

named John. John was born on 29 May 1825 in Ayot St Peter. The second child of Thomas and Jane was a daughter but very little is known of her. The third child was a son, Thomas ...'

With this method you can weave in as much detail as you wish, which would not normally be included in other more formal types of layout. It is important to write your history clearly and to make it interesting. It should not be a tedious roll call of names and dates. Punctuating the text with pictures and diagrams is a very good way of lightening the story. You can split your text into blocks that fit a page along with relevant pictures in a pleasing layout, such as the examples shown in fig. 127.

A combination of two layout methods might suit your requirements. Fig. 128 shows a combined narrative and drop-line pedigree chart. This is useful when one member of the family stands out from the rest with a very interesting life history or when an aspect of the family history needs lengthy elaboration.

When your research reaches epic proportions and one chart will not suffice for all that is to be included, it is time to make it into a book. Both the drop-line and narrative-style pedigrees can be used in book form, as is explained in the next chapter.

Chapter 7
A Family Tree Book

To write the family history in book form has many advantages. Photographs and clippings can be included. The book can be stored away easily and carried about to show the rest of the family. There are no problems with prolonged exposure to light and the family tree will remain in excellent condition provided that care is taken when handling.

The narrative pedigree is especially suitable for book use as it is a simple matter to continue the columns of text from page to page until everything you wish is included. Drop-line pedigrees can also be adapted to fit the pages of a book. The chart is broken into page-sized parts and the connecting lines can be taken to the edge of each page and referenced onto another page so that it is easy for your readers to follow the lines from one page to the next.

Page proportions

A portrait format, where the width of the page is less than the height, is most appropriate for narrative books (fig. 129). A landscape format, in which the width is greater than the height, is better for the drop-line style where you need maximum width to include all members of each generation on horizontal lines across the page (fig. 130).

Choosing a paper

Paper for a book must have both front and reverse of a quality good enough to be written upon. Test any paper by writing on both sides. The reverse side of many laid papers is sometimes too uneven for lettering. Smooth surfaced papers are better for books as the two sides are more uniform. Laid paper should have the grain running from left to right rather than from top to bottom; this is a detail and need not be adhered to if your chosen proportions make this impractical. If the paper is watermarked it looks neater to have the watermark the correct way round.

The size of your pages can be governed by the paper you choose. A large

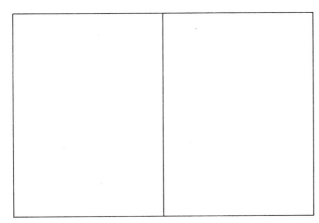

Fig. 129   Portrait format

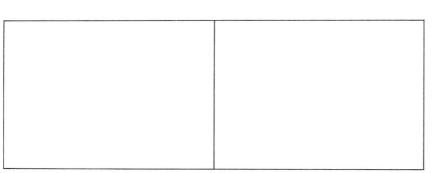

Fig. 130   Landscape format

(a)

(b)

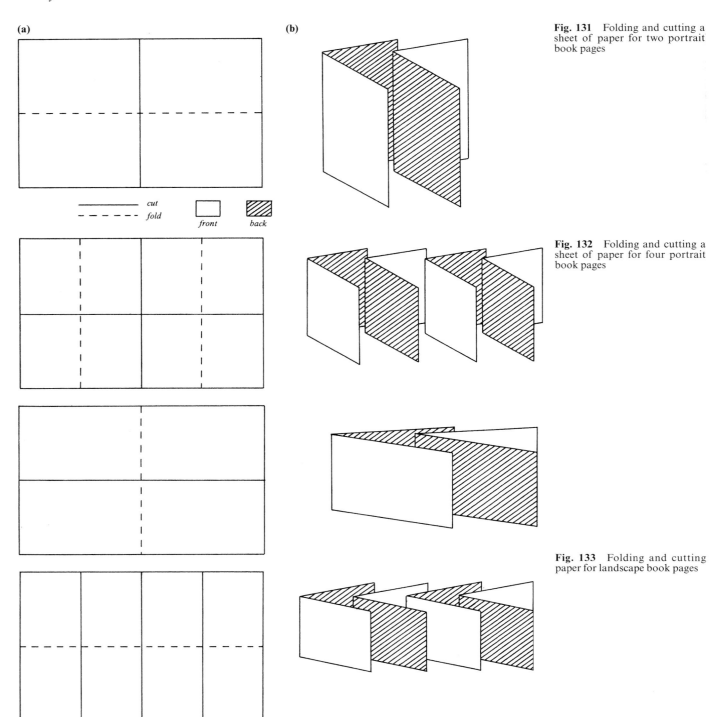

cut
fold
front
back

Fig. 131 Folding and cutting a sheet of paper for two portrait book pages

Fig. 132 Folding and cutting a sheet of paper for four portrait book pages

Fig. 133 Folding and cutting paper for landscape book pages

sheet of good quality paper may be cut into two or four equal pieces which are folded together so that the front side always faces another front side and reverse side faces reverse side. If the sheet is divided in two, as shown in fig. 131a, then folded (fig.131b), it will give 8 sides of paper for the work. A sheet divided into four pieces will give 16 sides for the work (fig. 132). Cutting the paper in either of the ways shown will give portrait format pages. For landscape pages the paper should be cut as shown in fig. 133.

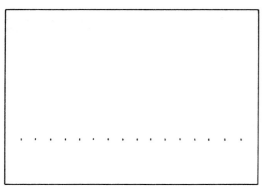

divide the page width into 16-18 equal parts, one part is then the unit of measurement to use for the margins

Fig. 134   Dividing up a page into equal portions to calculate margins.

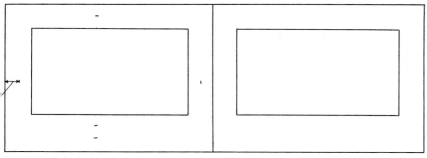

Fig. 135   Calculating margin proportions for each page

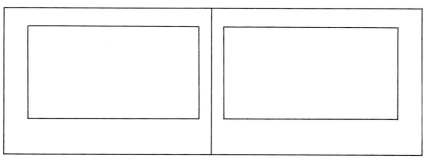

Fig. 136   Calculating margins as a double-page spread

Margins

Margins are required to frame the text and make it look well balanced on the page. They are also required because the edges of the page have most finger contact and so it is best to keep the text away from areas which will receive a lot of handling. Good margin proportions are achieved by dividing the width of the page into between sixteen and eighteen equal parts, as shown in fig. 134. (The exact number is a matter of personal preference; some people find wide margins give a very open appearance to the page whereas others prefer to see the text occupying a larger area.) One of these parts is the unit of measurement for calculating the margins. Top and side margins can be made equal or the top margin can be slightly narrower than the sides. Two units are used for the side margins and one and a half to two units for the top margin. If each of two open pages of a book is considered as a separate page then use two units on each side of the central fold (fig. 135). If the two open pages (a double-page spread) are considered as one whole page then the central margin can be the same width as the side margins so that one unit falls either side of the central fold (fig. 136). Fig. 135 uses two units for the top margin and 136 uses one and a half units. The choice is yours as to which combination of measurements best suits you. The bottom margin is always the largest as a bottom margin of equal or less depth than the top and sides tends to make the text look as if it is too far down the page. Three to four units are therefore used for the bottom margin.

Mark up a sheet of layout paper with the size of book page and calculate the proportions of the margins. For the sample book, which will be shown stage by stage, the size of the chosen paper is 70cm x 100cm. The book will use the drop-line style and so a landscape format is needed. The paper, cut in four, will give pages of size 25cm x 35cm (fig. 137).

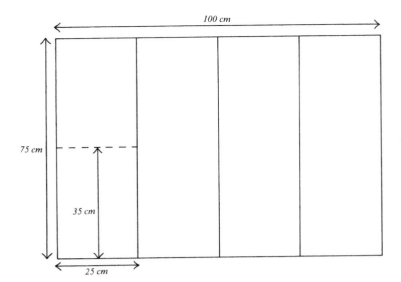

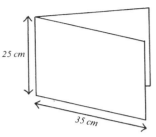

Fig. 137   Page sizes

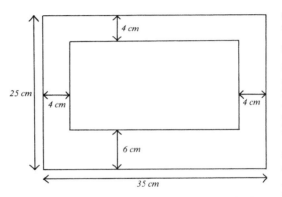

Fig. 138   Margin sizes

Dividing the page width into seventeen equal parts gives a unit of measurement of just over 2cm for calculating the margins. As 2cm will be close enough to make the proportions balanced, this figure can be used for ease in calculating. The sample page is shown in fig. 138 with correctly proportioned margins.

With the margins in place, next decide how you will distribute the text of your family history over the various pages. Fig. 139a shows the text intended for a family history book using the drop-line format and fig. 139b shows how it can be split into portions to occupy a series of pages. Use scrap paper to sketch out the names and plot roughly where you think the dividing lines can go so that there is about the right amount of text on each page. Fig. 140 shows the information

divided roughly across a set of pages. When deciding how to split your chart, try to keep family surname groups together on a page if possible, and go to another page when bringing in a new branch. Large families can be shown over double-page spreads so that a family group can be kept intact. Try different arrangements of the text until you reach a set of pages which work well. The order in which you place the different parts of the chart is not too important as each page will be cross-referenced to the page on which the chart continues. Do not worry about connecting the different pages at this stage. Concentrate on dividing the information into reasonable amounts for each page.

When you have ascertained how many sides of paper are needed for the text you can calculate how many pages and how many sheets of paper you will need. The number of pages must be a multiple of four as each new folded page you add will give you another four sides. In the example the text has been split into eight pages; but as there will also be a page for the title and a few pages for photographs and fly leaves, either twelve or sixteen pages will be used. Leave a few blank pages at the end of the book to add to the family tree at a later date. With that in mind, sixteen pages has been chosen for the example-book.

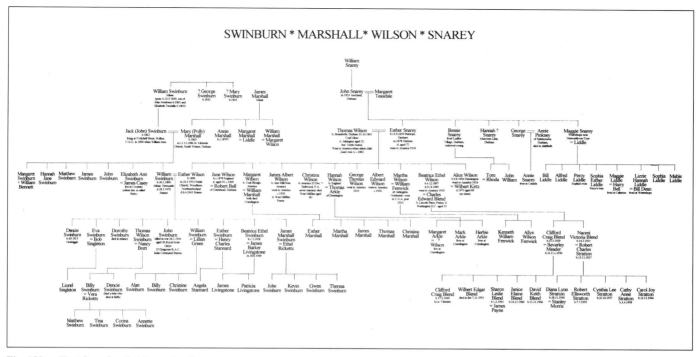

Fig. 139a   Text for a family history book

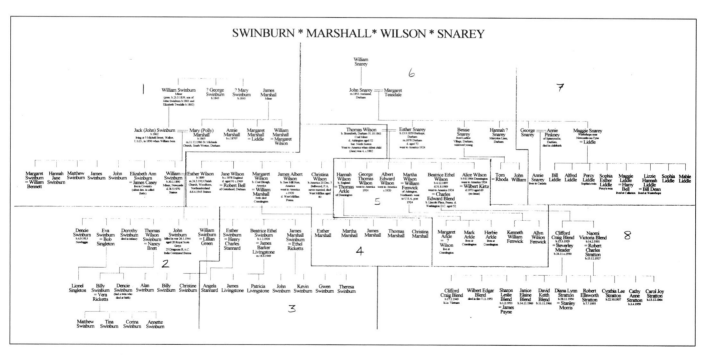

Fig. 139b   Text split into page-sized portions

Family Trees

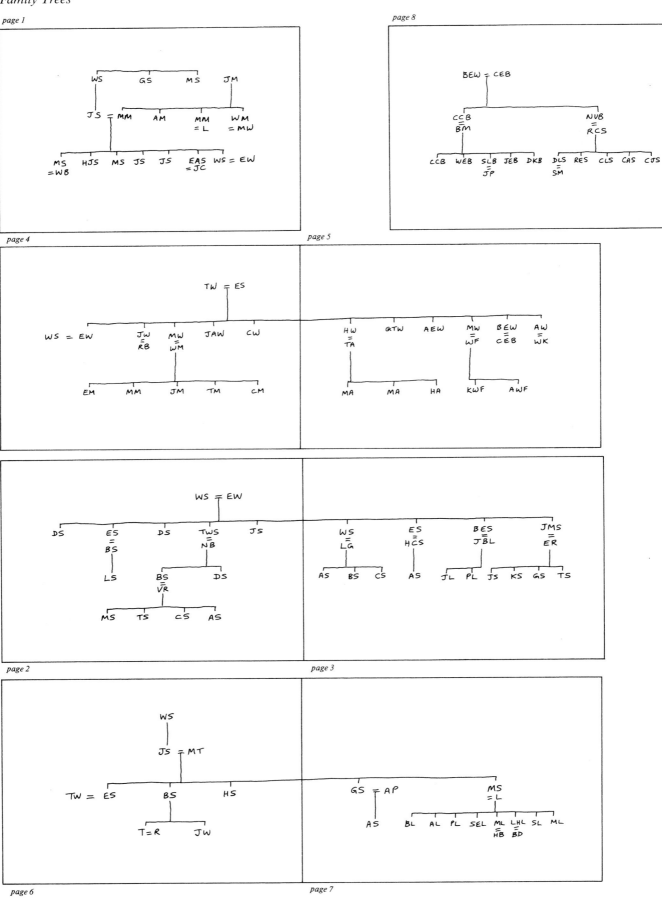

Fig. 141 Small-scale rough guide

Using a small-scale rough

It is very useful indeed to make up a small rough booklet to sort out the page order of the book. Fold together some small sheets of scrap paper – the number of sheets you intend to use – and then number each page in the top corner (fig. 141). In the example-book the pages are marked up, as shown in fig.142. Pages one and two must be left as blank pages or fly leaves (as described below). Page three is the title page so page four will be left blank as its reverse. Page five is the first text page and the text will also occupy pages six to twelve which are marked accordingly. Pages thirteen and fourteen will be set aside for photographs. Pages fifteen and sixteen must be left blank as end fly leaves.

The next step is to make a working draft of each page to determine your lettering sizes, space between generations, etc. The procedure for each page or double page spread is very similar to that required for an ordinary flat-sheet chart. The main difference is that pages must be linked together so that the chart can be followed from page to page. There are two ways in which this can be done. The first is to make the connecting lines run to the edge of each page and then begin again on the corresponding page at the same place, as shown in fig. 143a. A reference to the following page number can be written discreetly at the end of the line in the way in which atlases work. The second method requires writing some of the names a second time with small arrowed markers indicating the follow-on page (fig. 143b). Number the pages on your draft sheets and work out on to which page each part continues. Work through the rough drafts page by page using the steps given in chapter 2 on layout. If you are using the first method of cross-referencing the pages, given above, then match up the level of the connecting lines carefully from one page to another. Lines can be taken around the edge of the page so that they start again from the top of the page if necessary. Although the connecting lines run into the margins and the page references are written near the edge of the page, do not let the main text extend beyond the text area within the margins. Do not write the page reference numbers too close to the edge of each page as they will need to be trimmed later, and 2 or 3mm will be removed from some pages.

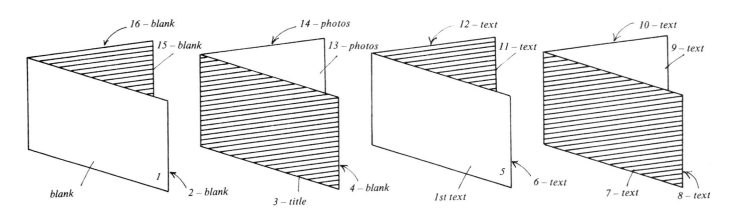

Fig. 142 Marking up the pages

Fig. 140 *(facing page)*
Text drafted out over a set of pages

Fig. 143 *(overleaf)*
(a) Drafts for pages using connecting lines;
(b) Drafts for pages using cross-referencing arrows

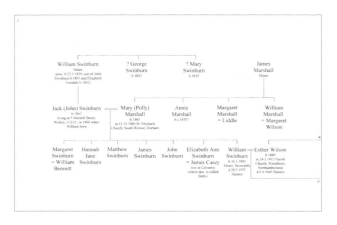

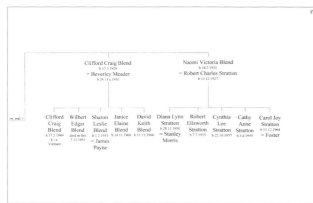

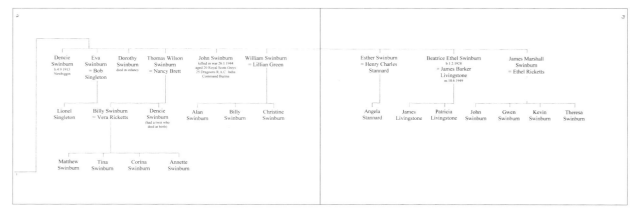

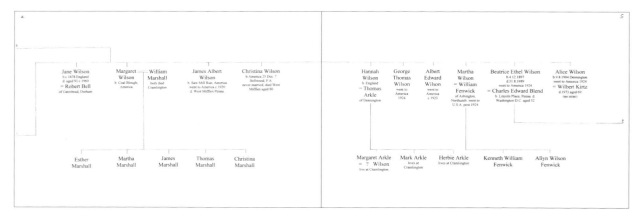

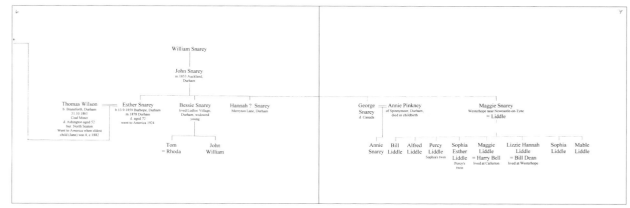

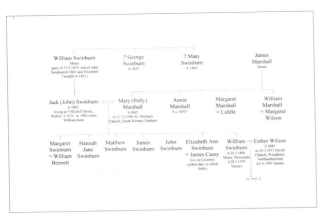

Panel 1

William Swinburn
Miner
(poss. b 23.5.1839, son of John
Swinburn b 1801 and Elizabeth
Tweddle b 1802)

? George Swinburn b 1843   ? Mary Swinburn b 1845   James Marshall Miner

Jack (John) Swinburn b.1862 living at 5 Michell Street, Walker, U.S.D. on 1890 when William born
= Mary (Polly) Marshall b.1865 m.11.12.1886 St. Michaels Church, South Westoe, Durham
Annie Marshall b.c.1870?
Margaret Marshall = Liddle
William Marshall = Margaret Wilson

Margaret Swinburn = William Bennett   Hannah Jane Swinburn   Matthew Swinburn   James Swinburn   John Swinburn   Elizabeth Ann Swinburn = James Casey (live in Coventry) (eldest dau. is called Betty)   William Swinburn b.30.1.1890 Miner, Newcastle d.28.5.1970 Staines = Esther Wilson b 1889 m.24.3.1913 Parish Church, Woodhorn, Northumberland d.6.4.1945 Staines [see page 2]

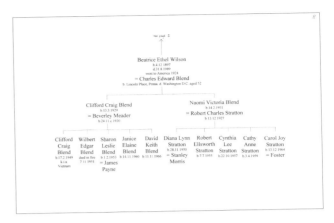

Panel 8

[see page 5]

Beatrice Ethel Wilson b.4.12.1897 d.31.8.1989 went to America 1924 = Charles Edward Blend b. Lincoln Place, Penna. d. Washington D.C. aged 52

Clifford Craig Blend b.13.3.1929 = Beverley Meader b.24.11.c.1930
Naomi Victoria Blend b.14.2.1931 = Robert Charles Stratton b.13.12.1927

Clifford Craig Blend b.17.2.1949 k.i.a Vietnam   Wilbert Edgar Blend b.7.11.1951   Sharon Leslie Blend b.1.2.1953 = James Payne   Janice Elaine Blend b.14.11.1960   David Keith Blend b.11.11.1966   Diana Lynn Stratton b.28.11.1950 = Stanley Morris   Robert Ellsworth Stratton b.7.7.1955   Cynthia Lee Stratton b.22.10.1957   Cathy Anne Stratton b.3.4.1959   Carol Joy Stratton b.13.12.1964 = Foster

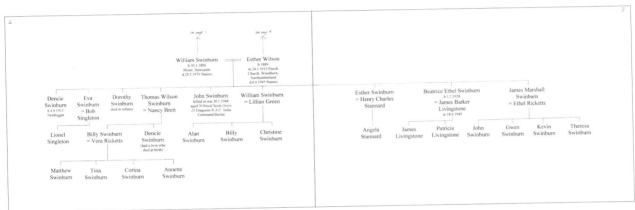

Panel 2

[see page 1]   [see page 4]

William Swinburn b.30.1.1890 Miner, Newcastle d.28.5.1970 Staines
= Esther Wilson b 1889 m.24.3.1913 Parish Church, Woodhorn, Northumberland d.6.4.1945 Staines

Dencie Swinburn b.4.9.1913 Newbiggin   Eva Swinburn = Bob Singleton   Dorothy Swinburn died in infancy   Thomas Wilson Swinburn = Nancy Brett   John Swinburn killed in war 26.1.1944 aged 20 Royal Scots Greys 25 Dragoons R.A.C. India Command Burma   William Swinburn = Lillian Green

Esther Swinburn = Henry Charles Stannard   Beatrice Ethel Swinburn b.1.2.1928 = James Barker Livingstone m.18.6.1949   James Marshall Swinburn = Ethel Ricketts

Lionel Singleton   Billy Swinburn = Vera Ricketts   Dencie Swinburn (had a twin who died at birth)   Alan Swinburn   Billy Swinburn   Christine Swinburn

Angela Stannard   James Livingstone   Patricia Livingstone   John Swinburn   Gwen Swinburn   Kevin Swinburn   Theresa Swinburn

Matthew Swinburn   Tina Swinburn   Corina Swinburn   Annette Swinburn

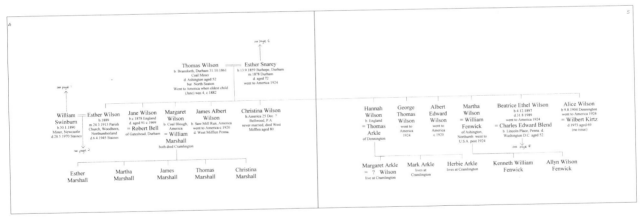

Panel 4

[see page 6]

Thomas Wilson b. Brandforth, Durham 31.10.1861 Coal Miner d. Ashington aged 52 bur. North Seaton Went to America when eldest child (Jane) was 4, c.1882
= Esther Snarey b.13.9.1859 Burhope, Durham m.1878 Durham d. aged 72 went to America 1924

[see page 2]

William Swinburn b.30.1.1890 Miner, Newcastle d.28.5.1970 Staines = Esther Wilson b.1889 m.24.3.1913 Parish Church, Woodhorn, Northumberland d.6.4.1945 Staines   Jane Wilson b.c.1878 England d. aged 91 c.1969 = Robert Bell of Gateshead, Durham   Margaret Wilson = William Marshall both died Cramlington   James Albert Wilson b. Coal Blough, America went to America c.1920 d. West Mifflen Penna.   Christina Wilson b. America 25 Dec. ? never married, died West Mifflen aged 80

Esther Marshall   Martha Marshall   James Marshall   Thomas Marshall   Christina Marshall

Panel 5

Hannah Wilson b. England = Thomas Arkle of Dennington   George Thomas Wilson went to America 1924   Albert Edward Wilson went to America c.1920   Martha Wilson = William Fenwick of Ashington, Northumb. went to U.S.A. post 1924   Beatrice Ethel Wilson b.4.12.1897 d.31.8.1989 went to America 1924 = Charles Edward Blend b. Lincoln Place, Penna. d. Washington D.C. aged 52 [see page 8]   Alice Wilson b.9.8.1904 Dennington went to America 1924 = Wilbert Kirtz d.1973 aged 69 (no issue)

Margaret Arkle = ? Wilson live at Cramlington   Mark Arkle lives at Cramlington   Herbie Arkle lives at Cramlington   Kenneth William Fenwick   Allyn Wilson Fenwick

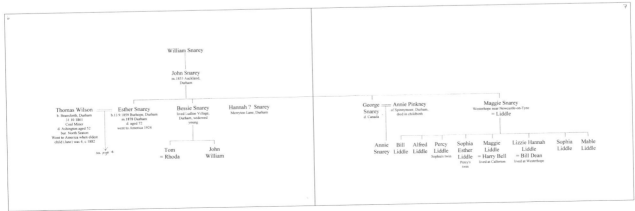

Panel 6

William Snarey
John Snarey m.1853 Auckland, Durham

Thomas Wilson b. Brandforth, Durham 31.10.1861 Coal Miner d. Ashington aged 52 bur. North Seaton Went to America when eldest child (Jane) was 4, c.1882 = Esther Snarey b.13.9.1859 Burhope, Durham m.1878 Durham d. aged 72 went to America 1924 [see page 4]   Bessie Snarey lived Ludloe Village, Durham, widowed young   Hannah ? Snarey Merryton Lane, Durham

Tom = Rhoda   John William

Panel 7

George Snarey d. Canada = Annie Pinkney of Spennymoor, Durham, died in childbirth   Maggie Snarey Westerhope near Newcastle-on-Tyne = Liddle

Annie Snarey   Bill Liddle   Alfred Liddle   Percy Liddle   Sophia Esther Liddle Sophia's twin (Percy's twin)   Maggie Liddle = Harry Bell lived at Callerton   Lizzie Hannah Liddle = Bill Dean lived at Westerhope   Sophia Liddle   Mable Liddle

Title

The title page of a book is the right-hand side of a double page spread with the left-hand page remaining blank as in the example book. A half title, which is usually a smaller, simplified version of the main title, is used on the preceding right-hand page. The title page of the book presents a good opportunity to introduce a little decorative design. Decide on the lettering style and layout of the title page and make a working draft, as for the other pages (fig. 144).

Adding photographs or illustrations

You should now have a full set of draft pages. If you are going to include illustrations on the text pages, you must work them into the text as you do your drafts and leave spaces for them. Photocopy the photographs and attach the copies to the draft pages so that you know exactly what is going where. If you are using separate pages for the photographs, as in the example-book, then they should also be planned at this stage (fig. 145). The draft pages now need to be joined back to back so that you can see which page needs to be written on the reverse side of which. Stick the pages together as shown in fig. 146 so that you have a complete draft of the contents of the book.

End papers and fly leaves

End papers are required at the front and back of the book if it has a hard cover. They are used for sticking the cover to the book. The paper chosen can be that used for the text or it can be a decorative paper. Marbled paper (available from Falkiner Fine Papers) is very attractive and suitable for this purpose, making a good robust paper for keeping the cover sturdily attached. You will need two sheets cut to the same size as the text sheets to go at the front and back of the book. They will be glued to the front

Fig. 144 Draft title page

and back fly leaves when the book has been stitched together.

Fly leaves are spare sheets of paper at either end of the book which come between the end papers and the first and last pages of the book. Their purpose is to act as 'margins' for the whole book but you must have at least one fly leaf at each end to fix the end papers to the book. How many you choose to include after this is a matter of personal preference. Some books begin with several blank fly leaves and they can be useful for writing dedications, attaching bookplates etc. Fly leaves should be of the same paper and the same size as the text pages. It will help if you add draft fly leaves to your working draft as they will become part of the main section or sections of the book and will be sewn together with them before binding. The end papers are not included in the sewing and must be kept separate.

Sections

If your book has many pages then it may be necessary to divide it into sections that are easier to sew than one large wedge of pages. If you are using a thick paper then you will want no more than four sheets to

Fig. 145 Draft photograph
pages

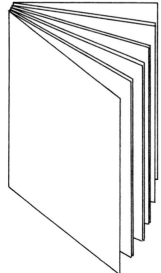

Fig. 146 Glueing together draft
pages

a section. If you have six sheets and decide to divide them into two sections three sheets thick, then your page numbering must be altered (fig. 147). If you need to do this, then make a new mini draft and renumber the two separate sections so that you will know how to fold and number the sheets for the book.

Writing the book

Cut the sheets of paper for the text pages and fly leaves to the correct size. Fold the pages in the correct direction to ensure that front sides match front sides and reverse sides match reverse sides. The sheets can be opened out again for working on but it will help to avoid errors if you can clearly see which way each page folds. Rule up the pages lightly with the margins and writing lines and mark the number of each page lightly in each corner. This is most important; there is nothing more frustrating than putting the book together and finding that the pages do not fall in the correct sequence. Write out the text page by page using a guard sheet as explained on page 11. Use your mini rough draft to make sure you write the correct text on the correct side of each folded sheet. Put in the connecting lines with a ruling pen. Mark in reference points for any cuttings, photographs etc. then carefully stick them into place using PVC glue or spray mount. Spray mount is an aerosol adhesive, available from art shops, ideal for this sort of work. Lay the picture face down on a sheet of paper and spray a thin coating over the whole surface. Wait a few minutes for the spray to become tacky then pick up the picture carefully and position it accurately on the page. If you are quick it is possible to peal off and reposition the picture if it is incorrectly placed. When all the pages are complete fold them and place them in the correct order in their sections.

Stitching the pages

To stitch the pages of a section of book together you will need binding thread and a suitable needle, which are available from Falkiner Fine Papers. For books with a spine up to 18cm long use three sewing holes; for longer spines, such as the book used in our sample, use five. Divide the length of the spine into six equal parts and make small pencil marks on the inside

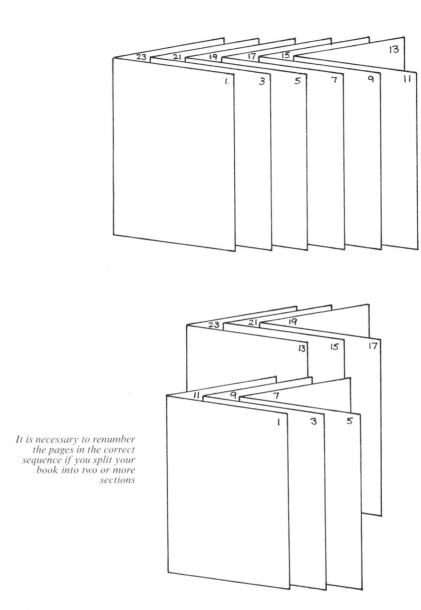

It is necessary to renumber the pages in the correct sequence if you split your book into two or more sections

Fig. 147 Altering page numbering for multi-sectioned books

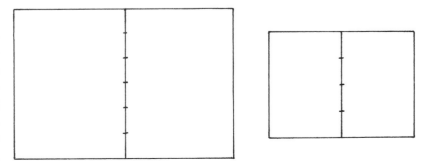

Fig. 148 Marking stitching holes

Fig. 149 Sewing sequence

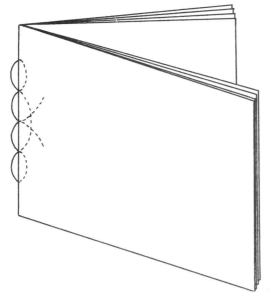

thread where necessary so that the whole length is fairly taut but not so tight as to buckle the pages. Tie together the two loose ends so that the two threads come either side of the centre strand and it is firmly tied down. Cut off the excess thread leaving about an inch on each end. When the sewing is finished, give the book a good pressing under a pile of heavy books for several hours so that the pages are pressed flat.

Binding a single section book with a flexible cover

If your book contains only a single section and you do not wish to go to the trouble of a hard cover, the book can be bound with a flexible but hard-wearing paper cover. Suitable binding paper is available from Falkiner Fine Papers, but any tough tear resistant paper will do. Papers which have woven threads running through them are ideal for this type of use. The cover should be cut so that it slightly overlaps the opening edges, as shown in fig. 150. Fold the cover around the book section before sewing. The cover can then be sewn into place with the rest of the pages. When pages are sewn together they will fan out slightly at the opposite end, so to neaten the edges they should be trimmed with a sharp knife. Use a Stanley knife, a metal rule and a piece of firm board (all available from hardware shops). Place the closed book on the board and clamp down the edge to be trimmed by pressing down the metal rule firmly with your hand where you want to cut. You should only need to

centre fold for each of the five holes (fig. 148). Take the sewing needle and, holding the book section together very carefully, push the needle through each hole so that it comes out of the other side and your sewing holes can be clearly seen on the spine. Now thread the needle with sewing thread about three times the length of the spine. Take the thread through the centre hole (fig. 149). Do not tie a knot in the end of the thread but make sure that the end is not pulled through. Stop pulling through with about 10cm of the end remaining and take care, as you thread the other holes, not to let the end slip nearer to or come through the first hole. Thread in the sequence shown, and be sure to avoid pushing the needle through the previous thread as you pass a second time through a hole. When you reach the end, pull the

Fig. 150 Overlap allowance for a flexible cover

3mm overlap for paper cover

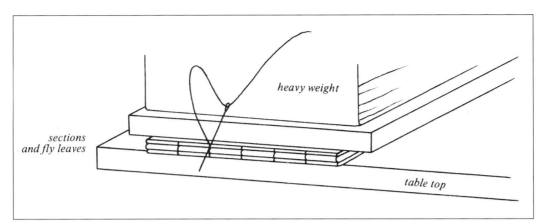

Fig. 151 Sewing together separate sections

trim a millimetre or two, so make sure to hold the rule firmly so that the knife cuts off the required amount. Keep drawing the knife blade along the edge until you have cut through the whole thickness of the book. You should have achieved a perfect straight edge to the end of the book.

Sewing together sections and fly leaves

Books with several sections must have them sewn together at the spine. When you have stitched each section as explained above, clamp them all together in the correct sequence under a heavy weight of books so that the edges protrude slightly (fig. 151). Sew the sections together with binding thread so that they are firmly attached. It is difficult to do this neatly when you have only a few sections to join together. As the thread will not be seen, the main aim is to make sure that the sections are firmly attached to each other while still allowing the book to open freely. It is worth making a dummy set of sections of blank pages on which you can practise sewing before launching into the proper book. If the width of the spine is more than 1cm it can be strengthened by pasting a strip of webbing (available from Falkiner Fine Papers) along the spine after sewing. Cut the webbing to exactly the same size as the spine, and give the spine a good application of glue. Allow the glue to dry

slightly so that it becomes tacky then press the webbing into place. Leave to dry before attaching the end papers, as for a single section book below.

Attaching the end papers

The end papers need to be stuck to each end of the book using PVC glue (available from Falkiner Fine Papers). You will also need a gluing brush or some small pieces of card, which can be used as spatulas for applying the glue, and several large sheets of clean scrap paper to be placed between the pages to prevent excess glue around the edges from sticking the wrong sheets together. Place the book on a sheet of scrap paper, then place another sheet between the top two leaves. Paste over the whole top sheet of the book making sure to give a good even coating right into the corners. Carefully remove the inner sheet of scrap paper with the excess glue and replace with a clean sheet. Lay the folded end paper into place. Lay another guard sheet on top of the end paper and press under a heavy weight of books. After a few hours, when the glue is dry, repeat the process with the second end paper at the other end of the book.

You now need to trim the edges of the book. Use a Stanley knife and metal rule and remove the minimum possible to achieve neat straight edges, in the manner described earlier for a flexible cover. You are now ready to start on the cover.

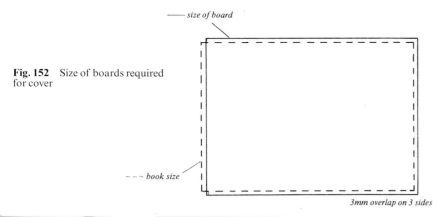

— size of board

Fig. 152 Size of boards required for cover

‑ ‑ ‑ book size

3mm overlap on 3 sides

Fig. 153 Binding cloth

Binding

Larger books require a hard cover to keep the pages in good condition and use boards for the front and back covers. Good quality millboard can be obtained from Falkiner Fine Papers. For the average book 3mm-thick board should be sufficient. If you have difficulty obtaining millboard, then hardboard, available from DIY shops, makes an adequate substitute. The cutting of the boards needs to be accurate so that the edges will be in line. The board must overlap the book on the three open sides but must be set in slightly from the spine; so measure the size required allowing a 3mm overlap around the protruding edges (fig. 152). Pencil the required dimensions onto the millboard then, holding a metal rule very steadily along the length of a cutting line, cut with

a sharp knife. You will not get through the board with a single stroke so be careful not to move the rule until the board has been cut right through or you will have an uneven edge. Place the cut boards together; if they are at all warped, make sure that the edges curve inwards to each other rather than outwards. Mark which is the front and which the back board so that you do not lay them wrongly when covering with the cloth.

Binding cloth (fig. 153) is available from Falkiner Fine Papers and is a very easy material to work with. Leather makes a beautiful covering for a book of this sort, but it needs to be carefully pared wherever it is stuck down and this is a very skilled process. It is recommended that you consult *Basic Bookbinding* by A.W. Lewis if you contemplate binding in leather.

The cloth for the cover is cut as shown in fig. 154. Measure the width of the spine of your book when the pages, fly leaves and boards are all held firmly together. Allow one and a half times the width of the spine in the centre of the cloth so that the spine of the cover will curve slightly when the book is open. Lay the two cover boards side by side on top of the cloth with the measured amount of spine gap between them. Mark each corner of the boards on the cloth so that they can be replaced quickly and accurately when pasting down the cloth. Mark a 5cm border around both boards for the turnover of the covering. Cut out the cloth and then replace the boards. Mark and then mitre the corners as shown, making the diagonals at 45 degrees to the edges of the boards and leaving a gap of 5mm between the corner and the diagonal cut so that the cloth will cover the edge of the board when folded. If you are using a dark coloured cloth, then you will need tailor's chalk (available from haberdashery shops) to make the marks, rather than a pencil.

PVC glue will be used for sticking the book cover together. Remove the

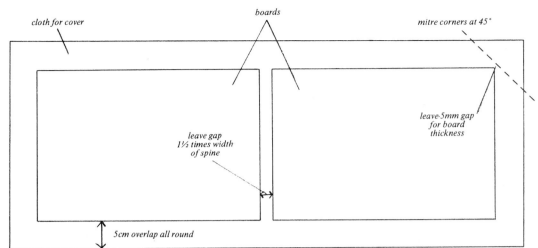

Fig. 154 Cutting binding cloth

cloth for cover

boards

mitre corners at 45°

leave 5mm gap
for board
thickness

leave gap
1½ times width
of spine

5cm overlap all round

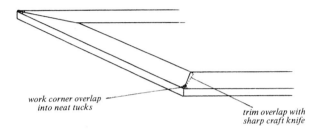

Fig. 155 Neatening the corners

work corner overlap
into neat tucks

trim overlap with
sharp craft knife

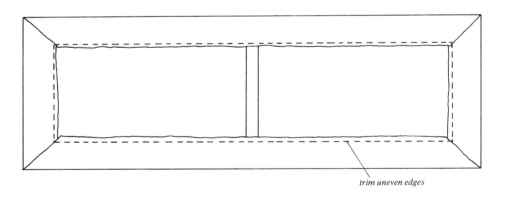

Fig. 156 Trimming the excess cloth

trim uneven edges

boards and paste the whole surface of the cloth. Replace the boards carefully on the marks and fold over the edges of the cloth, pressing them down carefully one by one. Make sure that they are sticking well and that the cloth is flat with no creases along the edges. Take care with the corners and work in the edges neatly so that you have a well finished corner, as shown in fig. 155. You can use a small knife to cut away any overlap between the two edges of cloth so that they lie neatly together. Finally, trim the uneven edges of the turnover so that they run parallel with the edges of the book (fig. 156). If the glue is still tacky, the excess pieces should peel off. Set the cover aside to dry.

When the cover is dry, lay it open on a clean sheet of paper. Take the book contents and lay them on the back cover so that the front end paper is ready to be stuck down. Place a sheet of clean scrap paper between the front end paper and the rest of the pages, then paste the whole surface of the end paper. Remove the scrap paper and carefully close the book cover so that the end paper sticks into place, taking great care to position it accurately. Gently open the book to check that the end paper is accurately in place and smooth it down with a bone folder so that it is lying flat. Insert a clean sheet between the cover and first page to prevent sticking, then close the book again. Place another clean sheet on top of the book, and press under a pile of heavy books whilst it dries. When the book is dry, open it out and make sure exactly where the back board of the cover will lie so that the spine will be correctly aligned and curved slightly. Place the book, open at the back end paper, on a clean sheet of paper with a clean sheet between the pages as before. Repeat the process with the back end paper. When the book is dry, take out the guard sheets and gently open the covers. Bend them back to form slight creases along the edges nearest the spine. The book should now open correctly each time it is used.

A title can be written on another piece of binding cloth to be stuck to the cover and pressed into place. Alternatively, the title can be painted directly onto the cover using acrylic paint. This is a water-based paint, available from most art shops, which is water resistant when dry. Figs. 157 and 158 show the finished book.

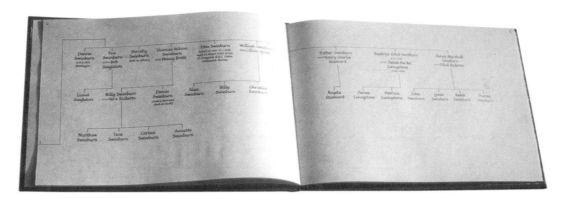

Fig. 157   Finished book open

Fig. 158   Finished book closed

Chapter 8
Display and Storage

There are various ways of displaying a family tree once it has been completed. The safest method is to frame the chart behind glass so that the paper or vellum is protected from smoke, moisture, finger marks and so on.

Frames

The choice of frame is a matter of personal taste and may also be governed by the decor of the room in which it is to hang and perhaps the cost. High street framers, who specialise in quickly produced, economically-priced frames, have a good range of mouldings to choose from (fig. 159). A stained wood or gold moulding with simple carving will suit many charts. More ornate carved mouldings, those using expensive woods or special finishes, can be obtained from specialist picture framers, but the cost can climb considerably when you look for something out of the ordinary. Frames are available in many colours, or one can be specially painted for you in a colour of your choice or with a special texture such as a marble or vellum effect. The moulding on frames usually slopes from thick on the outside to thin on the inside (fig. 160a) but it is also possible to get reverse mouldings which slope from narrow on the outside to thick on the inside edge (fig. 160b) and these can give a very pleasing effect on family trees. Charts can also be protected and hung with glass and clips only, as shown in fig. 161.

When choosing a frame bear in mind that generally the larger the piece the wider the frame moulding should be. Very large charts with narrow frames look unbalanced. With an average sized chart of perhaps 30" x 24" a frame of about 2"

Fig. 159 Frames are available in a wide range of colours and mouldings

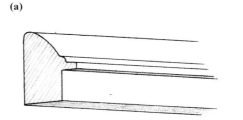

(a)

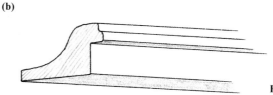

(b)

Fig. 160 (a) Standard frame moulding; (b) Reverse moulding

92

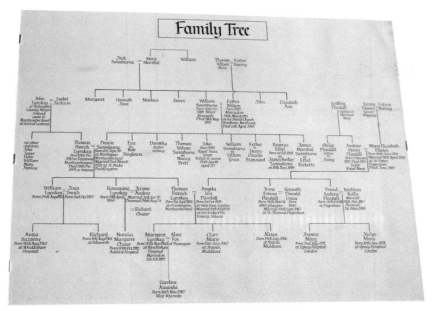

Fig. 161 Glass and clips

frame itself. If the board is thick enough it can take the place of a wooden slip. Some pieces of work lend themselves to this additional border. Charts with many illustrations benefit from a mount, whereas those with mainly text do not need an extra border. Framers will have a good choice of colours so that one can be found which will complement the work.

If it is likely that you may want to remove the work from the frame at some time to make additions or amendments, ask the framer to fix the backing board with moveable clips rather than tacks.

It is possible to have a frame with another chart mounted on the reverse side. This can be useful if, for artistic purposes or to limit the size, you did not include all the information you would have liked to put on the main chart. A lot of additional background information for people listed on the chart can be put onto another sheet mounted onto the reverse of the frame. As this side will not be seen except by anyone who expresses a particular interest in knowing more about the family, the information can be typed out neatly so that plenty of extra material can be included.

Charts on rollers

Another method of displaying or storing a chart is on a wooden roller. If you want to be able to roll and unroll your chart often, you must choose a paper for the work which is flexible and which will roll up easily in the correct direction. Some papers roll lengthways but not widthways or vice versa. You will also need to leave an extra 75-100mm of border at the top and bottom of your chart so that the roller and hanger can be attached. The roller may be specially made by a wood turner, but a cheaper alternative is to visit a do-it-yourself shop to find the materials to make it yourself. Lengths of wooden dowelling can be purchased in several thicknesses. A diameter of about 22mm is a good thickness for most charts. You

in width would provide a well balanced surround to the chart. Sizes of between 1in. and 1° in. in width will suit smaller charts. If you have a very small piece of work, sometimes the reverse is true and a very wide frame will make it look much more impressive, giving it an air of importance and visual appeal. This works with pieces containing a lot of very small text as the frame draws you to look more closely at the contents. Always ask the framer for his or her advice. On the other hand, if you have set your mind on a particular type of frame then do not be deterred from choosing it against the framer's judgement.

If your chart includes paintings, fit a slip of wood between the paper and the glass. A very thin, narrow strip of wood serves to keep the glass from lying against the work. This will prevent the paint adhering to the glass, which can sometimes happen, especially with metallic paints which are applied more thickly than ordinary paints. A slip also gives the whole frame extra thickness and a 'heavyweight' look which can work very well on large pieces. A gold slip looks very attractive with many plain wooden frames.

A coloured mount board can be used as a border around the work within the

should be able to find either pine or darker hardwood dowelling (fig. 162). For the ends of the roller you can buy wooden knobs of the same diameter which are attached to the ends of the dowelling pole with wood glue (fig. 163). You will also need a strip of wood about an inch wide for the top edge of the chart, to which you can attach a hanging cord. Narrow wooden border friezes with all sorts of attractive patterns, such as that shown in fig. 164, are widely available. A width of about 25mm would suit most charts and the thickness of the strip must be sufficient to take small pins knocked in about 5mm. The strip shown in fig. 164 was 7mm thick. The roller and top strip can be varnished and you can buy small tins in a variety of different coloured stains from DIY shops.

Your chart will benefit from being strengthened with a backing fabric. Buy a thin fine canvas-type material such as that shown in fig. 165. Tartalan or Permastiff are two types of suitable material which you might find in a local fabric shop. The canvas will be glued to the back of the work with PVC glue. You will also need some binding material for the top and bottom edges to strengthen them when they are attached to the roller and top strip. Use seam binding which you can buy from a haberdashery shop. You will need about 2 metres of 1 inch wide binding. About a metre of 6mm piping cord from a haberdashers will be needed. In addition the pieces of glued wood will need to be attached to the work with small pins or nails. Upholstery nails, which look like heavy duty drawing pins, work very well for the bottom roller. Fig. 166 shows some with an attractive daisy pattern. For the top piece small 13mm pin nails will be needed.

Before you begin sticking the canvas to your work, experiment first with spare pieces of canvas and the paper used for the work. Determine how much glue is required to make the canvas stick and

Fig. 162 Dowelling pole for roller

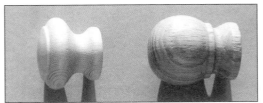

Fig. 163 Wooden end knobs

Fig. 164 Decorative wooden frieze for hanging strip

Fig. 165 Canvas backing fabric

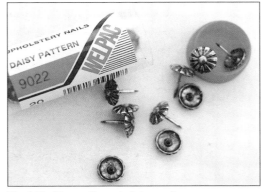

Fig. 166 Decorative upholstery nails

make sure that the chart will flex properly when stiffened.

When you are ready, measure and cut a piece of canvas slightly larger than the size of your chart so that there is an overlap of about 2cm on each side. Lay your chart face down on a clean sheet of paper and cover the whole surface with a thin even coating of glue. Use a piece of stiff card to spread the glue and make sure to coat the edges of the paper well. Carefully lay the canvas over the paper, pressing it down firmly to make sure that no creases occur and that it is completely attached. Remove the soiled underneath sheet and replace it with a clean sheet; then leave the chart to dry. A word of caution for those who have used paint on the chart as well as ink – the moisture from the glue can be sufficient to dampen the paint, so, when you are pressing down the canvas, use the minimum pressure to prevent the damp paint from adhering to the underneath paper. It will help, once you have spread the glue on the chart, if you replace the sheet of paper underneath with a sheet of blotting paper.

When the glue has dried, check that the canvas is well stuck down. If it is not, a second coating of glue can be applied over the canvas and allowed to dry. Trim the edges of the chart so that you remove the excess canvas. Cut two strips of seam binding slightly longer than the top and bottom edges of the chart. Glue a strip to each end, wrapping it carefully around both sides as shown in fig. 167. Leave to dry completely.

Cut a length of dowelling an inch longer than the width of the chart. Smooth the ends flat with fine sandpaper. Glue on the end knobs with wood glue. Cut a piece of top strip also an inch longer than the chart width. Give both strips of wood a few coats of varnish. The top piece of wood will have the hanging cord attached to it, which can be done either by attaching small ring hooks (available from hardware shops) or by drilling small holes at either end of the wood in the last half inch which overlaps the chart at each end (fig. 168).

When the varnish is dry the roller and top strip can be attached to the chart. Lay the chart on clean paper again and spread glue along the bottom binding strip. Press the roller down onto the binding strip and leave to dry. The binding strip will probably be quite firm and it is difficult to make it lie closely against the roller, but you can assist by fixing strips of masking tape around the roller and chart whilst it dries. It does not matter if the roller is not completely stuck down as the tacks will do the main job of holding the roller in place. When the glue is dry, knock in the upholstery tacks at regular intervals along the roller (fig. 169).

For the top end of the chart cut a piece of seam binding long enough to wrap around and tie the chart when it is rolled up (fig. 170a). Mark the centre of the top edge of the chart on the reverse side. Find the centre of the tying strip and sew it onto the bound edge (fig. 170b) with a needle and thread. Sew right through the edge of the chart, bringing all three thicknesses of seam binding and the chart firmly together. Spread glue along the front edge of the binding strip and press the top strip of wood into place. Heavy weights can be placed on top whilst it is drying. When it is dry, pin nails can be knocked in at regular intervals along the back of the wooden strip, but take care not to drive them too far in. When the pin has a good anchorage in the wood, bend the protruding part so that it lays flat against the wood. If you use ring hooks for the hanging cord, screw them in at either end of the hanging strip. Thread the cord through the rings or holes and tie the ends securely. The finished chart (fig. 171) can either be displayed permanently or kept rolled up.

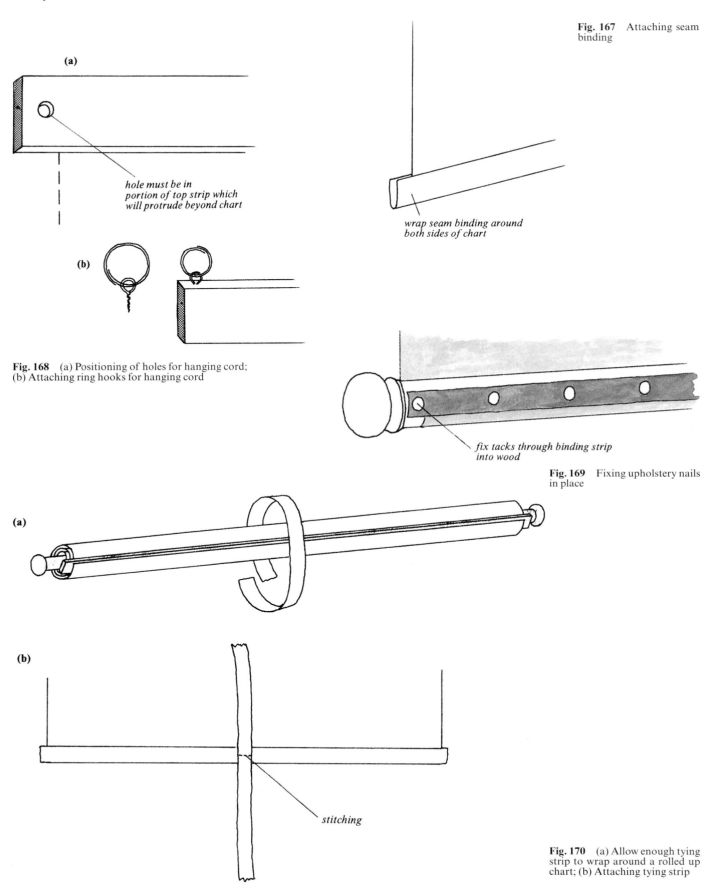

Fig. 167 Attaching seam binding

(a)

hole must be in portion of top strip which will protrude beyond chart

(b)

Fig. 168 (a) Positioning of holes for hanging cord; (b) Attaching ring hooks for hanging cord

wrap seam binding around both sides of chart

fix tacks through binding strip into wood

Fig. 169 Fixing upholstery nails in place

(a)

(b)

stitching

Fig. 170 (a) Allow enough tying strip to wrap around a rolled up chart; (b) Attaching tying strip

Fig. 171   Finished scroll

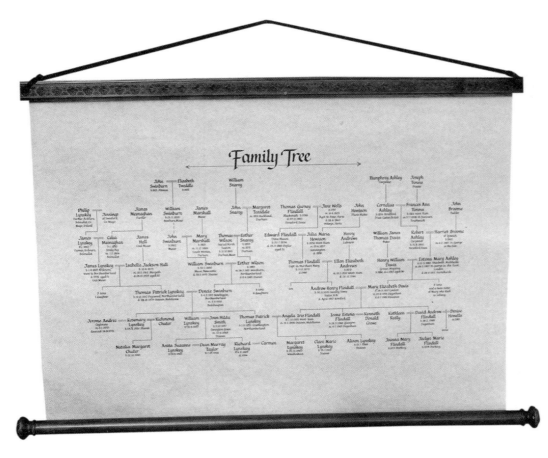

Storage

The worst fate that a family tree can suffer is to be kept stored folded up. As anyone who has studied old documents knows, the folds weaken the paper and leave the creases susceptible to tearing. If you intend to store your chart, it is best kept rolled in a tube. Strong cardboard tubes are not easy to come by and many are too narrow in diameter to take a large rolled chart. A good alternative is to store the chart in a length of plastic drain piping. DIY superstores sell 6 ft lengths and you can saw the length you require. Sandpaper the cut ends to remove the rough edges. Sometimes drainpipe can be rather dusty and grubby inside so first work a cloth or tissues around the inner surface to remove any dirt. You may be able to find end caps but, if not, use paper plugs at either end of the tube to protect the chart. The work can be further protected by wrapping it in acid free tissue available from Falkiner Fine Papers.

A book is the safest method for storing your family history, as the pages are kept out of the damaging effect of sunlight and changing atmospheric conditions. A danger books face is from careless use by their readers. When you were buying your paper for the family tree you should have taken into account the durability of the paper (see p.6). Hand-made papers last longer than those that are machine made and there are many archive and conservation grade papers which are made to last. You should still take care to handle the pages as little as possible and avoid rubbing your fingers across the page.

Reproduction

If your masterpiece impresses other members of the family who would like a copy, it is possible to acquire good quality prints, avoiding the necessity of writing the whole chart again (fig. 172). Extra black and white photocopies can be obtained from many printers and some stationers and art shops up to A0 (84cm x 119cm). Your artwork will need to be run through rollers in a large copying machine so make sure that the person operating the machine takes good care of your work. The cost is only a few pounds even for the largest size. Do not use this method if your chart is on vellum. Only allow a vellum chart to be copied if the method of reproduction involves lying the chart flat as on a normal A4 size copier.

Large colour copies up to A1 (59cm x 84cm) in size can be obtained from some colour printers and photocopy companies. Again be wary if you have used vellum for the chart, as some methods use heat and this will make vellum warp a great deal. The skin will return again into shape when it cools but often with an added kink or

two. The colours of colour copies, like photographs, vary greatly and some of the colours on a chart may not be a good match for your original; bear this in mind if you are looking for an exact copy. Your chart can be reproduced in a different size from the original, so that mini versions can be sent to relatives.

You can photograph the chart and have large prints produced. It is difficult to get every part of a large chart in focus and a specialist photographer is usually required for a good job.

I hope that the instruction in this book will lead to many more well produced and longlasting family tree charts. Genealogy is a very rewarding hobby and the more people take an interest in it and record their findings, the better it is for future generations who may want to know about their ancestors.

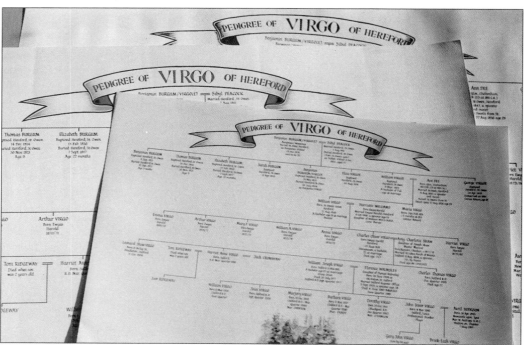

Fig. 172   Reproduction

List of Suppliers

Falkiner Fine Papers Ltd
76 Southampton Row
London. WC1B 4AR

papers, vellum, pounce, bookbinding materials, nibs, pens, ink

William Cowley
Parchment Works
97 Caldecot Street
Newport Pagnell
Bucks. MK16 0DB

vellum, parchment, pounce

Winsor & Newton
Whitefriars Avenue
Wealdstone
Harrow Middx. HA3 5RH

'Designers Gouache' paint, brushes

Rexel Art & Leisure Products
Gatehouse Road
Aylesbury
Bucks. HP19 3DT

William Mitchell pens

T. N. Lawrence
119 Clerkenwell Road
London. EC1R 5BY

papers, brushes, ink

Rotring U.K.
Building One
GEC Estate
Wembley
Middx. HA9 7PY

Rotring pens and lettering stencils

Further Reading

Genealogy

Begley, Donal F., *Irish Genealogy: A Record Finder* (Heraldic Artists Ltd., 1981)

Cole, Jean and Church, Rosemary, 'In and Around Record Repositories in Great Britain and Ireland', *Family Tree Magazine* (1992)

Cox, Jane and Padfield, Timothy, *Tracing Your Ancestors in the Public Record Office* (HMSO)

FitzHugh, Terrick V.H., *The Dictionary of Genealogy: A Guide to British Ancestry Research* (Alphabooks, 1985)

Gibson, J.S.W., *Marriage, Census and Other Indexes for Family Historians* (FFHS)

Gibson, Jeremy and Peskett, Pamela, *Record Offices: How to Find Them* (FFHS, 1985)

Hamilton-Edwards, G., *In Search of Ancestry* (Phillimore, 1983)

Hamilton-Edwards, G., *In Search of Scottish Ancestry* (Phillimore, 1983)

Hey, David, *The Oxford Guide to Family History* (OUP, 1995)

McLaughlin, Eve, *Parish Registers* (FFHS)

McLaughlin, Eve, *St Catherine's House* (FFHS)

McLaughlin, Eve, *Somerset House Wills* (FFHS)

McLaughlin, Eve, *The Censuses, 1841-1891* (FFHS)

Pelling, George, *Beginning Your Family History* (Countryside Books, 1980)

Heraldry

Burke, Sir Bernard, *Burkes General Armory* (Heraldry Today, 1984)

Civic and Corporate Heraldry, a Dictionary of Impersonal Arms (Heraldry Today, 1971)

Fox-Davies, A.C., *A Complete Guide to Heraldry* (Bonanza Books, 1978)

Woodcock, Thomas and Robinson, John Martin, *The Oxford Guide to Heraldry* (OUP, 1988)

Woodward, John and Burnett, George, *Woodward's Treatise on Heraldry British and Foreign* (David and Charles, 1969)

General

Lewis, A.W., *Basic Bookbinding* (Dover Publications, 1957)

Lynskey, Marie, *Creative Calligraphy* (Thorsons, 1988)

The Calligrapher's Handbook (A & C Black, 1985)

Periodicals

Family Tree Magazine
The Genealogists' Magazine
Family History

Index